Presented To:

_____

From:

_____

Date:

_____

GLIMPSES OF AN
INVISIBLE GOD
for Women

Quiet Reflections to
Refresh and Restore Your Soul

HONOR
BOOKS

07 06 05 04 03   10 9 8 7 6 5 4 3 2 1

Glimpses of an Invisible God for Women
ISBN 1-56292-872-4
Copyright © 2003 by Honor Books
An Imprint of Cook Communications Ministries
P.O. Box 55388
Tulsa, Oklahoma 74155

Manuscript written by Vicki Kuyper and Stephen Parolini

Introduction

More than ever before, people are searching—longing for a deeper relationship with God. Most have no problem recognizing His distinguished hand in the bright hues of the rainbow, the magnificent grandeur of the night sky, the breathtaking vistas of the Grand Canyon. But many of these seekers are hoping for more. *Is He present in the routine moments of my everyday life?* they wonder.

If you have been asking that question, *Glimpses of an Invisible God* is just for you. As you move through its pages, you will enjoy the little stories about people just like you, people who discover that God is really there for them. We have supplied scriptures for each story to guide your reading. Also, you will have an opportunity to learn what can happen when God enters into both the great and small details of your life.

We know you will be blessed as you discover the depth of God's love for you and His commitment to walk with you moment by moment.

You will find Him if you seek
Him with all your heart.

DEUTERONOMY 4:29 NKJV

Those who seek the Lord lack no good thing.

PSALM 34:10 NIV

And after he (Jesus) had dismissed
the crowds, he went up to the
mountain by himself to pray.

MATTHEW 14:23 RSV

Coffee and the Quiet

Jenny loved 2:15 in the afternoon. Benjamin was napping, and John wouldn't be home from school for another hour. The dishes were done, so she sat and savored a cup of coffee. She knew just how many sips it would take until John would come bounding through the door. On sip number seven, she paused to reflect on what her neighbor had said weeks ago: "God is ready when you are. He's right there waiting."

But where? Jenny wondered as she began sip number eight. Then she paused, finally realizing the obvious. *Of course,* she thought. *I don't have to search for You in some exotic, faraway place. You've been right here with me all along!*

Jenny set her cup on the table and smiled through her tears. "God . . . I want to know You," she whispered. And right there in that moment, her relationship with God began in earnest.

God is waiting for you as well. Reach out to Him today!

To pray does not only mean to seek help; it also means to seek Him.

Clearly, you are a God who
works behind the scenes.

ISAIAH 45:15 THE MESSAGE

Come and see what God has done,
how awesome his works in man's behalf.

PSALM 66:5 NIV

For I know the plans I have for you,
says the Lord. They are plans
for good and not for evil,
to give you a future and a hope.

JEREMIAH 29:11 TLB

Surprised by Joy

"God, I hate this job. This office building is so big that I just feel lost in the crowd. I can't do this much longer! I feel so alone and discouraged," Kristen prayed. "Oh, and, uh, thank you for this food."

Kristen opened her eyes and began to eat just as she had for the past two weeks—alone. She was startled by a tap on her shoulder. "Kristen! I didn't know you worked here!"

"Peg?" Kristen looked up in disbelief into the eyes of her high school friend. "I can't believe it's you! I just started here a couple of weeks ago." She continued shyly, "I guess I'm still a newcomer."

"Not for long," Peg replied with a smile. "Let me introduce you to the gang."

Consider things like unexpected phone calls, chance meetings, and surprise glimpses of beauty. Are they merely coincidences, or are they Glimpses of an Invisible God? What do you think?

A coincidence is a small miracle where God prefers to remain anonymous.

Where you are right now is God's place for you.
Live and obey and love and believe right there.

1 CORINTHIANS 7:17 THE MESSAGE

Trust in the Lord with all your heart; do not
depend on your own understanding. Seek his
will in all you do, and he will direct your paths.

PROVERBS 3:5 NIRV

And my God will meet all your needs according
to his glorious riches in Christ Jesus.

PHILIPPIANS 4:19 NIV

*The Lord has turned all
our sunsets into sunrises.*

Home Is Where Our Father Is

Donna had to leave it all behind, again—her job, her friends, her relatives, even her obstetrician. And in her second trimester, Dr. Parker's face would have been a welcome sight. But her husband's latest transfer had taken them thousands of miles away from all things safe and familiar.

"Our writer's group was just getting off the ground, God," she complained. "And what about Sandy? I really liked having a friend who was pregnant at the same time." Donna burst into tears—again! But the sound of the doorbell forced her to hurriedly dry her eyes.

She opened the door to find a young woman standing on her step, self-consciously adjusting her maternity top. "I'm sorry to bother you," the woman said with a smile. "I was just excited to see you move in. I've been praying for someone to talk to!"

God makes a provision for every circumstance. Open your heart, and trust Him with the circumstances in your life.

Pour out your heart like water
in the presence of the Lord.

LAMENTATIONS 2:19 NIV

Trust in him at all times, O people;
pour out your hearts to him,
for God is our refuge.

PSALM 62:8 NIV

Save me, O God, because I have come to
you for refuge. I said to him, "You are
my Lord; I have no other help but yours."

PSALM 16:2 TLB

Here Comes the Flood

Susan spent a frustrating and tearful hour on the phone with her mother. Then her son's teacher called to tell her Sean was failing geometry. Her husband, Gary, left a message that he was looking at another all-nighter at the office. The dog got into the pantry again. And it wasn't even noon. She was ready to explode.

It was time to find a quiet place where she could open the floodgates and let God know how she felt. She knew that God didn't mind when she cried or even yelled. He could handle her frustration, so she let it all go!

When she had said all she had to say, Susan took a little more time—a few moments—to let Him fill her with good things like peace, patience, love, and wisdom.

Are there some things you need to talk to God about? Be honest—He can take it. And telling Him will help you make it!

God takes life's pieces and gives us unbroken peace.

My soul is downcast within me;
therefore I will remember you.

PSALM 42:6 NIV

I remember you while I'm lying in bed.
I think about you through the night.

PSALM 63:6 NCV

I will remember the works of the Lord;
Surely I will remember Your wonders of old.

PSALM 77:11 NKJV

Forever Blessed

Depression had been part of Dorothy's life as far back as she could remember. Even when it seemed nothing was really wrong, she still felt something just wasn't right. For several years she'd taken antidepressants and spent time with a therapist.

After a period of time, Dorothy's friends noticed that she seemed to have a new-found joy. When they asked what made the change in her life, Dorothy couldn't help but talk about her "blessings" book.

"Every morning I spend some time reading the Psalms," Dorothy explained. "I can relate to all those emotional ups and downs. Then, I write down everything I'm thankful for in my journal. If it's a tough morning, I go back and read what God has done for me in the past. That always brings to mind something new I need to say 'Thank You' for. Those few moments with God give me the courage to face the day with a positive outlook."

Consider a "blessings" book of your own.

Counting your blessings divides your sorrow.

The unfolding of thy words gives light.

PSALM 119:130 RSV

Your word is a lamp to my feet
and a light for my path.

PSALM 119:105 NIV

Let the words of Christ, in all their richness,
live in your hearts and make you wise.

COLOSSIANS 3:16 NIRV

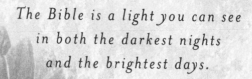

*The Bible is a light you can see
in both the darkest nights
and the brightest days.*

Discovery

Brian shuffled along the basement floor, flashlight darting left, then right. "I know it's here somewhere. . . . " The circle of light stopped on a large chest. As soon as he opened it, the memories began to spill out.

A tear pooled in his eye as he flipped through his wedding album. As he turned another page, his flashlight dropped into the chest and rolled against the back of the wooden box. The beam fixed on a black leather book.

Brian picked up his wife's Bible, dusted it off, and tucked it under his arm. He sadly recalled the last and only time he'd joined his wife at church: her funeral. Brian carefully replaced the albums and closed the chest. As he reached the stairs, he wondered if the Bible would shed some light on his world. By the time he reached the main floor, he was counting on it.

Is there a Bible in your home that needs to be dusted off?

You will keep in perfect peace all who trust
in you, whose thoughts are fixed on you!

ISAIAH 26:3 NLT

I have told you these things, so that
in me (Jesus) you may have peace.

JOHN 16:33 NIV

For he is our peace, who hath made
both one, and hath broken down the
middle wall of partition between us.

EPHESIANS 2:14 KJV

A Question of Perspective

Watching her children grow reminded Sarah of what it was like to be a child herself—always asking questions. "Why is the grass green?" "Why don't fish drown?" "Why is thunder so loud?" As an adult, Sarah just accepted that there were questions she would never have the answers to, like, "Did life just begin by accident?" "What happened to my mom after she died?" "Does what I do really make any difference in this world?"

When a friend mentioned to her that the Bible had some of the answers she was looking for, Sarah began to read. She surprisingly found not only answers, but hope and a renewed passion for living.

There were still things she didn't understand, but the more Sarah learned about God, the more she trusted that He knew every answer.

A few glimpses of an invisible God can bring peace to your heart, and joy to your life, as well.

Other books were given for our information; the Bible was given for our transformation.

As a mother comforts her child,
so will I comfort you.

ISAIAH 66:13 NIV

He has not despised my cries of deep despair;
he has not turned and walked away.
When I cried to him, he heard and came.

PSALM 22:24 TLB

He heals the broken-hearted and
binds up their wounds, curing
their pains, and their sorrows.

PSALM 147:3 AMP

At Home in a Parent's Arms

Lisa turned off the light and crawled into bed. It was only 7:30, but that was the longest day she could handle during the past few weeks. Ron understood. He just didn't know how to help. Lisa learned she was pregnant just days before the miscarriage. But that was long enough for her to realize how much she wanted to be a mother—and how much she could love someone she'd never met.

The doctor had said that miscarriages at that stage of pregnancy were common and happened every day, but that was no comfort; Lisa's disappointment and grief were very personal.

So every night she crawled into bed to talk to God for a few moments about how much it hurt. She knew God could still hold her baby in His arms, even if she could not. And in this difficult time, He held Lisa in His arms, as well.

God is closest to those whose hearts are broken.

Are you hurting? If so, God's arms are always open for you.

Whatever you do, work at it will all your heart,
as working for the Lord, not for men.

COLOSSIANS 3:23 NIV

For you shall eat the fruit of the labor of your
hands; happy, blessed, fortunate, enviable
shall you be, and it shall be well with you.

PSALM 128:2 AMP

People who work hard sleep well.

ECCLESIASTES 5:12 NIRV

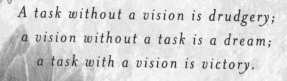

*A task without a vision is drudgery;
a vision without a task is a dream;
a task with a vision is victory.*

No Labor Lost

Donna walked to the back entrance of the hotel. *Even if I walked through the front door, people wouldn't really see me,* she thought. After all, she was just a maid. The work was hard, and the pay wasn't great, but the benefits really helped her family. And the morning schedule allowed her to be with her kids after school. It was a job—not her dream job, but it helped make ends meet.

Each day, Donna's work began before she opened the door marked "Maintenance." As she walked through the parking lot each morning, she put her day in God's hands. She prayed for His strength, joy, and perspective. As she worked, she pretended she was cleaning God's house, making it perfect just for Him. At quitting time, Donna was always proud of what she accomplished. And she felt sure her Heavenly Father was too.

Have you placed your day in God's hands?

Dear friends, let us love one another,
for love comes from God. Everyone who
loves has been born of God and knows God.

1 JOHN 4:7 NIV

Love your neighbor as yourself.

MATTHEW 19:19 NIRV

My prayer for you is that you will
overflow more and more with love for others.

PHILIPPIANS 1:9 TLB

24

Each Precious Moment

There are a few moments in life when everything seems perfect—when the list for the school play is posted, and your name is across from the lead role. Then there's that time when you realize your lab partner thinks you're oh-so-much-more-beautiful than the crystalline formations at the bottom of the test tube.

How about the split-second realization that the most wonderful person in the world is now officially your spouse? Or those "are you sure this is my child?" moments that come in just the right time to brighten an otherwise overcast day?

But the best moments always seem to have something to do with love: the love of a friend, a spouse, a child, and God's love. That's because true love is something much greater than we are. It's a taste of the eternal. And those perfect moments? They're a glimpse of the paradise we were created for.

Where love reigns, the very joy of heaven itself is felt.

Blessed are the peacemakers.

MATTHEW 5:9 NIV

A soft answer turns away wrath.

PROVERBS 15:1 AMP

Those who are peacemakers will plant seeds
of peace and reap a harvest of goodness.

JAMES 3:18 TLB

Fighting Frustration

"How can anyone call this fast food?" muttered Sela. She'd been in line for a long time, and she was in a hurry to get back to work. She glanced at the woman working behind the counter and noticed that she seemed on the verge of tears. Sela could feel the tension in the restaurant growing, and her heart quickly changed from annoyance to compassion. It takes less time to pray than to complain, she thought to herself, and it works so much better.

"Lord, please help that woman," Sela prayed. It was just one short line, but she knew that didn't matter to God. When she made it to the front of the line, she ordered her usual. Then with a gentle smile she said, "You're doing a great job handling all of these people."

The woman said softly, "Thanks. Two workers called in sick this morning. So, I'm just doing the best I can as fast as I can!"

Prayer makes you part of the solution, not part of the problem.

Prayer will defuse even your most volatile situations.

For whoever does the will of my
Father in heaven is my brother,
and sister, and mother.

MATTHEW 12:50 RSV

෨ᗙ

I take joy in doing your will, my God.

PSALM 40:8 NIRV

෨ᗙ

Our Father in heaven, hallowed be Your name.
Your kingdom come. Your will be done.

LUKE 11:2 NKJV

*Not as I will, but as thou wilt.
To be able to say these words and
truly mean them is the highest point
we can ever hope to attain.*

Holy Ground

"Look at this place!" Mona's mother said as she got out of the car. "Do you really want to work here after all you've sacrificed to make it this far?"

Mona's parents had pictured her with a profitable practice back in Maryland after Mona completed her medical degree. But here she was, settling in rural Tennessee. The small house in the woods was exactly where Mona wanted to be, near the people who needed her most. Despite the peeling paint, she saw what her mother did not—a place of physical and spiritual healing.

"It may not look like much, Mom," Mona told her softly. "But God brought me here, and that makes it holy ground. More than anything else, I need to know His presence is with me."

Her mother looked up at the old house one more time and then turned to Mona. "You're right," she said with a smile.

Are you exactly where God wants you to be?

I've refined you, but not without
fire, like silver. I've tested you
in the furnace of affliction.

ISAIAH 48:10 THE MESSAGE

Because the Lord God helps me,
I will not be dismayed; therefore,
I have set my face like flint to do his will,
and I know that I will triumph.

ISAIAH 50:7 TLB

When doubts filled my mind, your comfort
gave me renewed hope and cheer.

PSALM 94:19 NIRV

Change of Plans

Since the accident, Kelli spent months in bed, feeling totally useless. Physical therapy was painful, but at least it made her feel like she was accomplishing something. The rest of the time, a full-time nurse and a network of friends met her needs. It's not that she wasn't grateful for the help; she'd never had to rely on anyone other than herself.

Kelli found plenty of time to talk to God, but "talk" wasn't all she did. She yelled, questioned, cried, and eventually even offered thanks. Over the months, she came to understand that God loved her, even when her life didn't seem "useful." And she watched how God used that insight to soften her heart toward Him, as well as toward others.

God's love for us is based on His grace rather than our usefulness. If you are feeling a sense of helplessness, relax and rely on Him.

Pain teaches lessons that joy cannot.

How priceless is your unfailing love!

PSALM 36:7 NIV

I have loved you, says the Lord.

MALACHI 1:2 NKJV

For God so greatly loved and dearly
prized the world that He even gave up
His only begotten Son.

JOHN 3:16 AMP

Can't Buy That

Sarah couldn't stop staring at the ring on her finger. *I'm going to be married! I'm going to be married!* The same words continued to spin around her head, selfishly leaving no room for any others. Mike's smile widened as he watched her study the light dancing off the diamond. He was sure he'd made the perfect choice.

"This must have cost a fortune!" Sarah said, half-hoping he'd freely share the dollar figure, half-hoping she'd never know.

"I'll never tell," he replied. "But even if it had cost a million dollars, it would be just a tiny symbol of how much I love you."

Sarah felt fortunate to have Mike for a boyfriend—no—fiancé! "I want my love for you to reflect in some small way the immeasurable love God has for us," he continued. "It is priceless."

God loves each of us as if there were only one of us.

God's love is priceless, and He's offering it to you today. Will you receive it?

Since my youth, O God, you have taught me,
and to this day I declare your marvelous deeds.

PSALM 71:17 NIV

Come, my children, and listen to me,
and I will teach you the fear of the Lord.

PSALM 34:11 NIRV

All your children shall be taught by the Lord,
and great shall be the peace of your children.

ISAIAH 54:13 NKJV

*The flowers of all our tomorrows
are held in the seeds of today.*

Work of Heart

As Rhonda prepared to leave for her grandmother's funeral, she noticed the cross-stitch hanging in her entryway. The stitches were uneven, and a few of the knots had long ago pulled through, but Rhonda was just a kid when her grandmother had patiently helped her complete it.

Her grandmother had taught her much over the years—not only how to sew on buttons and make the best brownies, but also how to set aside time each day to talk to God. When she would spend the night at her grandmother's house, Rhonda always knew that when she awoke, she'd find Nana in her favorite chair with her Bible. Now, Rhonda had her own chair and her own time with God.

Not everyone can look back on a heritage of faith. But throughout your childhood, God was there, whether you knew it or not. Take time to teach a child about God's love today.

We do not know what we ought to pray for,
but the Spirit himself intercedes for us
with groans that words cannot express.

ROMANS 8:26 NIV

Because He has inclined His ear to me,
therefore will I call upon Him as long as I live.

PSALM 116:2 AMP

But we will give ourselves continually to
prayer, and to the ministry of the word.

ACTS 6:4 NKJV

Speechless

The tears had finally stopped, but Lauren's sobbing had not. Her child was desperately ill. She knew God still worked miracles, but she wondered if she even had the right to ask. She lay in bed, exhausted, but sleep wouldn't come. Before now, she'd never felt pain this deep, a sense of helplessness and confusion that left her almost unable to speak. All she could do was breathe.

But that was enough. God still heard her prayer, even though Lauren hadn't spoken a word. He heard the longings of her heart, and He reached out in love.

Prayer is communication that goes beyond words. When you feel you can't possibly talk to God, you may already be doing just that. Can you remember a time that left you speechless, but still aware of God's presence? Is there anyone at this place right now whom you could be praying for?

Even when there are no words, God still understands the question.

Ever since we first heard about you we have kept on praying and asking God to help you understand what he wants you to do.

COLOSSIANS 1:9 TLB

Ever since I first heard of your strong faith . . . I have never stopped thanking God for you. I pray for you constantly.

EPHESIANS 1:15-16 NIRV

I make mention of you always in my prayers.

ROMANS 1:9 NKJV

Sealed with a Prayer

All it took was a stamp and five minutes of Rachel's time, but Gail acted as if she had received the Hope Diamond. Rachel had no way of knowing what a tough time Gail was going through.

They'd been friends forever, but now with families of their own, keeping in touch had been reduced to a quick note at the bottom of their Christmas cards. When God brought Gail to mind, Rachel knew she had to do more than pray; she had to give a gift of her time.

Whether it's a phone call, an e-mail, or the ever-increasingly rare treasure of a personal letter, a few unexpected words of encouragement can work wonders. Perhaps God wants you to come alongside someone who's lonely. It's amazing what God can do through a simple act inspired by a heart that's attentive to Him. Whose name is He whispering to you today?

No one is useless in this world who lightens the burden of it for anyone else.

May the favor of the Lord our God rest upon
us; establish the work of our hands for us.

PSALM 90:17 NIV

For we are His workmanship, created in Christ
Jesus for good works, which God prepared
beforehand that we should walk in them.

EPHESIANS 2:10 NKJV

God will generously provide all you need.
Then you will always have everything you need
and plenty left over to share with others.

2 CORINTHIANS 9:8 NLT

*Charity is the scope of
all God's commands.*

Self-service

Gloria glanced at the line of bedraggled humanity—and sighed. She'd volunteered at the soup kitchen because a friend mentioned what a gratifying job it was. Gloria found it tedious and depressing. Anyone could scoop spaghetti. Big deal.

"God bless you," someone said, and the words caused Gloria to actually look at the person she was serving. There stood a woman about her age.

"Uh, you're welcome," Gloria stuttered. Suddenly she felt hot with shame. God could turn anything, even the simple words of a homeless person, into a blessing. In a fleeting second, Gloria prayed that God would use her time to bless others, in any way He saw fit. Suddenly, the job didn't seem so tedious after all.

Working through your own power and in your own selfish motives works against success and blessing, not for it. Whatever you find yourself doing today, ask God to take your efforts and turn them into something more.

I will keep you safe from your own people
and also from those who are not Jewish.
I am sending you to them to open their eyes so
that they may turn away from darkness to the
light, away from the power of Satan and to
God. Then their sins can be forgiven, and
they can have a place with those people who
have been made holy by believing in me.

ACTS 26:17-18 NCV

The Spirit of the Sovereign Lord is on me,
because the Lord has anointed me to
preach good news to the poor.

ISAIAH 61:1 NIV

For preaching the Good News is
not something I can boast about.
I am compelled by God to do it.

2 CORINTHIANS 9:16 NIRV

Soaking in It

"I get it! I finally get it!" Sandy shouted as she ran around the table and embraced Karen. Truly it was a wonderful moment. Though she'd gone to church for years, only now did Sandy realize that God wanted to have a personal relationship with her. Imagine! She could barely contain herself.

"I want to learn everything," Sandy said, looking directly into Karen's eyes. "I want to soak up all there is to know. Will you help me?" Tears mingled with giggles as she settled back into her chair at Karen's kitchen table.

"I will, Sandy. As long as you help me," answered Karen.

"Me help you—?" Sandy smiled quizzically. "But how? I don't know anything."

"It's not what you know," said Karen. "It's your excitement. I want to feel that again. We can help each other. Deal?"

"It's a deal!"

Is your relationship with God lacking excitement? If so, share it with someone—the flame will burn again.

It is a bad thing to be satisfied spiritually.

I praise you because I am fearfully
and wonderfully made.

PSALM 139:14 NIV

For the Lord sees not as man sees; for the
man looks on the outward appearance,
but the Lord looks on the heart.

1 SAMUEL 16:7 AMP

Charm is deceitful and beauty is
passing, but a woman who fears
the Lord, she shall be praised.

PROVERBS 31:30 NKJV

Comparison Shopping

Josie slid into her bubble bath, feeling like she'd hit the jackpot. Today, the mailman brought two fashion magazines and three new spring catalogs. Shopping while soaking—could a Friday night get any better than this? She could stay here for hours. *A hand-embroidered cardigan . . . crimson pumps . . . a taupe silk suit . . . I'd really feel beautiful in this,* she thought.

Then she felt the nudge of God's voice inside. *You're already beautiful,* she felt Him saying. In an instant, Josie realized the real reason she wanted that suit. She wanted to look like the model wearing it. She had always believed that with just the right outfit, she'd finally be beautiful. But somehow, she began to understand that God had created her to be who she was, no more and no less. In His eyes, she was already beautiful.

Do you struggle to feel beautiful? Look at yourself in God's mirror.

> *Let each man think himself an act of God, his mind a thought of God, his life a breath of God.*

When you give it to them, they gather
it up; when you open your hand,
they are satisfied with good things.

PSALM 104:28 NIV

My grace is sufficient for you.

2 CORINTHIANS 12:9 RSV

The Lord will guide you continually, and
satisfy your desire with good things,
and make your bones strong; and you
shall be like a watered garden, like a
spring of water, whose waters fail not.

ISAIAH 58:11 RSV

*If God maintains sun and
planets in bright and ordered
beauty, He can keep us.*

Just in Time

When Mandy and Tim sat at the dinner table, it wasn't to eat a great meal, though they'd had plenty of those. It was to draw thick black lines through budget items they could live without. "Cable? Gone. Health club? Outta here. Two dinners out a month? Strike 'em."

Mandy and Tim tried their hardest to smile. It wasn't easy. Without Tim's salary, life would be difficult for a little while—maybe a long while, if the economy didn't improve.

"We still have each other," Tim said.

"And we still have our faith," added Mandy. "What else do we need?"

"Nothing," Tim responded quickly, mainly because it seemed like the right thing to say. But suddenly he began to grasp the truth in it all. They wouldn't go hungry. They had a roof over their heads. He would work again. And every day they'd enjoy the richness of a relationship with God and with one another— nothing was more important than that.

Even to your old age and gray hairs
I am he, I am he who will sustain you.

ISAIAH 46:4 NIV

And now that I am old and gray,
don't forsake me. Give me time to tell
this new generation (and their children too)
about all your mighty miracles.

PSALM 71:18 TLB

You are my God. My times are in Your hands.

PSALM 31:14-15 AMP

Facing the Future

At Haven Glen, the doors of the tenants' rooms were like a personal gallery. Some used them to post calendars or treasured photos; others displayed original artwork or seasonal decorations. But the decor on Mae's door hadn't changed since she'd moved into the rest home five years ago.

On the wall a poster hung bearing the words, "I am He who will sustain you." Any time Mae went in or out of her door, she'd read those words to herself and smile. It's not that life was easy at ninety-two, but as Mae loved to remind her friends at Haven Glen, "At our age, every day's a blessing!"

Life can feel like a blessing, or a curse, at any age. A lot of it has to do with your attitude. How do you view growing older? How does knowing that God will be with you affect your view of aging? If you don't know, it's time to find out.

Every season of life holds its own abundant harvest.

Know that the Lord is God. It is he
who made us, and we are his; we are
his people, the sheep of his pasture.

PSALM 100:3 NIV

But as for me, oh Lord, deal with me
. . . as one who bears your name.

PSALM 109:21 TLB

How precious also are thy thoughts unto me,
O God! How great is the sum of them!
If I should count them,
they are more in number than the sand.

PSALM 139: 17-18 KJV

Smiling Down

From an early age, Tina knew she would become someone special. At first, she was going to wear ballet slippers and dance on a huge stage in front of an adoring audience. Later, she was certain she'd be the first woman to walk on the moon. Just last year, she followed a path that would lead her to the state Senate.

But things changed. Tina stopped making her plans and instead asked God to direct her steps and make her life fruitful. Soon after, she landed a job as program coordinator for a local youth organization. The pay wasn't great—the accolades, few. She didn't have a stage, but she did have a platform for influencing the lives of teenagers. Tina had become someone special. She had found her purpose in life.

In God's eyes, you are special. And if you ask Him, He will do for you what He did for Tina.

The engineer of the universe has made me part of His whole design.

Do not be anxious about anything, but in
everything, by prayer and petition, with
thanksgiving, present your requests to God.

PHILIPPIANS 4:6 NIV

Because he bends down and listens,
I will pray as long as I breathe.

PSALM 116:2 TLB

Be patient in tribulation,
be constant in prayer.

ROMANS 12:12 RSV

*Whate'er we leave to God,
God does. And blesses us.*

Shifting Gears

Driving anyone's car other than her own always left Marilyn feeling uneasy. How she ended up driving a rental car through the overcrowded streets of Mexico City was almost a calamity of errors. But here she was. Marilyn had virtually memorized the street map so she could navigate her way to the bank through the maze of one-way streets. Now, all she had to do was park.

"God, I feel silly asking this," Marilyn prayed, "but I need your peace—and a parking spot I can get into!" A truck abruptly pulled out in front of her car. After slamming on her brakes, she noticed the driver had just vacated an oversized spot along the curb right across from the bank. Marilyn took a moment to breathe and to offer thanks.

Prayer isn't reserved for life-and-death situations. If you're anxious, talk to God. He won't always change your circumstances, but His peace and presence will certainly change your focus.

Choose this day whom you will serve. . . .
As for me and my house,
we will serve the Lord.

JOSHUA 24:15 RSV

Let us pursue the things which make
for peace and the things by
which one may edify another.

ROMANS 14:19 NKJV

Be joyful always; pray continually;
give thanks in all circumstances,
for this is God's will for you in Christ Jesus.

1 THESSALONIANS 5:16-17 NIV

Starting Out Right

Martin and Kendra had waited for this moment for nearly a year. Oddly enough, that was about six months longer than Kendra's parents had hoped for. "Since when do parents encourage you to get married sooner, rather than later?" Martin had asked.

"They probably love you even more than I do," Kendra had replied.

As Kendra walked down the aisle, she seemed to drift on air. *How much more beautiful could a woman be than this?* Martin wondered. He hoped he could keep it together for the solo he'd planned.

As she stood beside him, Kendra felt a brief moment of doubt. *Is this right? Are we too young?* she wondered. Then she heard him singing. "As for me and my house, we will serve the Lord. . . ." Martin sang the words with passion and conviction—and instantly, her doubts vanished.

Give God first place in your marriage, and God will help you maintain it.

> *The best marriages are those where the partners look through each other to God.*

Whatever is true, whatever is noble,
whatever is right, whatever is pure,
whatever is lovely, whatever is admirable—
if anything is excellent or praiseworthy—
think about such things.

PHILIPPIANS 4:8 NIV

I will remember the works of the Lord . . .
I will also meditate on all Your work,
and talk of Your deeds.

PSALM 77:11-12 NKJV

May the words of my mouth and the thoughts
of my heart be pleasing to you,
O Lord, my rock and my redeemer.

PSALM 19:14 NIRV

Food for Thought

Shelly munched on her popcorn and chatted with her friends while they waited for the movie to start. She didn't know much about the plot, but when her friends from work had invited her to the theater, she had jumped at the chance. After a tough work-week, she was ready for a little fun.

It wasn't long after the opening credits that Shelly started feeling uncomfortable. She couldn't figure out whether the sex, violence, or language was the most offensive. But she was sure of one thing—she needed to leave. "I'll meet you in the lobby," she whispered to her friends. When she got out into the light, she was surprised to see Christina right behind her.

"I'm so glad you left when you did," Christina said. "I was too embarrassed to do it alone."

Garbage in, garbage out—what's true for your computer goes for your mind as well.

Man's mind is the Holy of Holies, and to admit evil thoughts is like setting up an idol in the temple.

The Lord longs to be gracious to you.

ISAIAH 30:18 NIV

I finally admitted all my sins to you and
stopped trying to hide them. I said to myself,
"I will confess them to the Lord."
And you forgave me! All my guilt is gone.

PSALM 32:5 TLB

For if ye forgive men their trespasses,
your heavenly Father will also forgive you.

MATTHEW 6:14 KJV

Our God has a big eraser.

Finding Forgiveness

Lucy had never felt she was really doing anything wrong, at least not back in high school. But now, after getting to know God, she saw what she'd done in a different light, and it wasn't a very flattering picture. Countless times she'd gone to God and apologized, but she never felt "clean." Her friends talked about the blessings God brought their way, but Lucy felt as though she deserved nothing. Instead, it seemed as if she'd be paying God back for the rest of her life.

Then she met Mark. He loved her, in spite of her past. But it wasn't until she heard the words "for better or worse" on their wedding day that Lucy caught a glimpse of what unconditional love and forgiveness were all about. She'd finally found a place of acceptance with both Mark and with God.

Once you've asked God for forgiveness, you're clean in His eyes, no matter how you feel.

God treat us kindly. You're our only hope.
First thing in the morning, be there for us!

ISAIAH 33:2 THE MESSAGE

In the morning, O Lord, you hear my voice;
in the morning I lay my requests before you
and wait in expectation.

PSALM 5:3 NIV

Morning by morning he
(God) wakens, he wakens my ear
to hear as those who are taught.

ISAIAH 50:4 RSV

Day Break

Mona had always been a morning person. Even as a kid, when her brother slept in until noon, she was up with the birds. She liked the feeling of being on her own, alone with the quiet. After all these years, morning still filled her with that same type of joy. But this morning seemed extra special. Last night she'd prayed with a friend for God to come into her life. When she awoke this morning and saw the sunrise, Mona could have sworn she heard God whisper, "Good morning, Mona; I love you."

She immediately decided she would begin each morning with the words, "Good morning, Lord; I love you." Even when the day ahead wasn't one she was really looking forward to, it made her smile just to know she could always count on God and His love, to be there with the sunrise.

When was the last time you said "Good Morning" to God?

Have breakfast with God, and start your day off right.

If you make yourselves at home
with me and my words are at home in
you, you can be sure that whatever you
ask will be listened to and acted upon.

JOHN 15:7 THE MESSAGE

Ask and it will be given to you;
seek and you will find; knock and
the door will be opened to you.

MATTHEW 7:7 NIV

We have confidence toward God.
And whatever we ask we receive from Him,
because we keep His commandments and do
those things which are pleasing in His sight.

1 JOHN 3:22 NKJV

Is Anybody Listening?

Julia opened the door of her son Kevin's room and sighed. Not that she really expected he would have cleaned it, but she had asked—three times. She kicked at a pile of dirty socks, then shut the door again. It was better not to look.

Some days, Julia felt that trying to communicate with teenagers was like talking to her houseplants—a total waste of time. "If, just once, someone would actually listen to me!" she grumbled. *I will,* she felt God reply.

Imagine if you only had to say something once to be heard. Now imagine not only being heard, but also understood and responded to. God is not only listening, but also ready to act when you speak to Him. He's not your personal genie, ready to fulfill your every wish, but He works through your prayers to bring about the fulfillment of His purposes in your life. How can you make yourself more "at home" with Him?

Prayer is the key of Heaven; faith is the hand that turns it.

Blessed are those whose strength is in you,
who have set their hearts on pilgrimage.

PSALM 84:5 NIV

Forgetting the past and looking forward
to what lies ahead, I strain to reach the
end of the race and receive the prize.

PHILIPPIANS 3:13-14 TLB

The steadfast love of the Lord never ceases,
his mercies never come to an end; they are
new every morning; great is thy faithfulness.

LAMENTATIONS 3:22-23 RSV

Man is born broken.
He lives by mending.
The grace of God is glue.

Repeat Offender

"If brains were dynamite, she wouldn't have enough to blow her nose!" Kristi remarked. Her comment about the new temporary employee elicited laughter from everyone at the lunch table, but as soon as she'd said it, Kristi began mentally kicking herself.

Just this morning, she'd talked to God about how her sarcasm was getting out of control. She tried not to cut others down, but some people just left themselves wide open; or so she rationalized. Here it was, barely noon, and Kristi was apologizing again. "Okay, God," she prayed, "This is it! I'm going to quit cutting people down, or die trying!"

The truth is, everyone's going to die trying. Trying to change ingrained habits or dysfunctional behavior is an ongoing process, even when you're leaning on God's strength for help. Don't beat yourself up when you fail. God extends grace and forgiveness, not a paddle and a dunce cap.

My times are in your hands.

PSALM 31:15 NIV

Turn me away from wanting
any other plan than yours.
Revive my heart toward you.
Reassure me that your promises are for me.

PSALM 119:37 TLB

Trust in the Lord with all your heart;
do not depend on your own understanding.

PROVERBS 3:5 NIRV

Celebrating the Present

Rosa had already thumbed through every magazine in the waiting room. She'd arrived ten minutes earlier, but today it felt like an eternity. The doctor had already seen the test results. It didn't seem fair that he should know before she did whether she was going to live or die. All Rosa could do was wait.

She absent-mindedly began to watch the fish in the tank nearby. *Such beauty in simplicity,* she thought. Rosa had discovered that the fear of limited tomorrows often provides a renewed appreciation for the blessing of each new day. And right now, she was enjoying this moment. An unexpected sense of peace began to replace her fear. The doctor may know the test results, thought Rosa, but only God really knows what lies ahead of me. I can trust Him with whatever that is.

How you face life affects how you'll face death. Where are you placing your trust today?

This moment is a gift to be unwrapped with eager hands.

Wait for the Lord; be strong and
take heart and wait for the Lord.

PSALM 27:14 NIV

Those who sow tears shall reap joy. Yes,
they go out weeping, carrying seed for sowing,
and return singing, carrying their sheaves.

PSALM 126:5-6 TLB

I will wait on the Lord . . .
and I will hope in Him.

ISAIAH 8:17 NKJV

Persevering in Prayer

Ming stood by the front window tightly clutching her small sack of belongings, waiting. As Tess walked up the front steps of the orphanage, she caught sight of Ming. The waiting was over. After years of longing, infertility testing, and adoption paperwork, she and her husband would finally have a child to call their own.

As the door opened, Tess was surprised that her sense of awe ran even deeper than her joy. After years of praying for a child, God's answer had sent Tess halfway around the world. As she knelt down to give three-year-old Ming a hug, she thanked God. To think, if she'd been able to conceive on her own, they never would have met. She couldn't imagine loving any child more than she did her beautiful new daughter.

Instead of a holding pattern, waiting is often God's growing pattern.

Are you waiting for an answer to prayer that seems as though it will never come? Don't give up. God's timing often holds unexpected blessing.

In Your presence is fullness of joy.

PSALM 16:11 NKJV

❧

I have loved you, O my people, with an
everlasting love; with lovingkindness
I have drawn you to me.

JEREMIAH 31:3 TLB

❧

Set me in your presence forever.

PSALM 41:12 NIV

*Let your religion be
less of a theory and
more of a love affair.*

Quiet Timezzzzzz

Tina took her Bible off the shelf, just as she did almost every morning. She tried to never skip her quiet time, but lately she had realized something was missing. Every word she read seemed boring, every prayer repetitive. God seemed a million miles away. She sighed, read a chapter, then left the room unchanged.

Suppose someone wanted to spend time with you every day. Now, suppose you went to the same place, did the same things, and had the same conversation over and over again. Boring, huh? Why put your relationship with God in this same type of a box?

Shake things up a bit. Write God a letter. Just sit and listen. Take a walk. Sing a song. Use a Bible commentary. Read a book on prayer. Write your own Psalm. Talk to God aloud. Don't give up. He loves you more than you know, and He wants to be part of your life, not just your routine.

It is good to be near God.

PSALM 73:28 NIV

Sing psalms, hymns, and spiritual songs
to God with thankful hearts.

COLOSSIANS 3:16 NIRV

Bless the Lord, O my soul;
and all that is within me,
bless His holy name!

PSALM 103:1 NKJV

72

Gimme! Gimme!

"Lord, please bless Katie as she leaves for school, Sarah as she goes for her doctor appointment, Rob as he's looking for a new job, those people near that earthquake in South America somewhere, me as I try to stay on my diet and . . . ."

Sometimes, prayer can sound like a grocery list of requests. It's true that God says you can ask Him for anything, but relationship isn't built on what someone else can do for you. It's founded on mutual love and respect. God's generosity is unlimited, and His love for you is unconditional, but He longs to be more than a source for unlimited favors.

Take time today to draw close to God, without asking for anything. Tell Him how much He means to you. Thank Him for the abundance He brings to your life. Why not bless your Heavenly Father today with the simple joy of your presence?

Live near to God and so all things will appear to you little in comparison with eternal realities.

Praise be to the God . . . who comforts us
in all our troubles, so that we can comfort
those in any trouble with the comfort
we ourselves have received from God.

2 CORINTHIANS 1:3-4 NIV

Three of Job's friends heard of
the tragedy he had suffered, they got
together and traveled from their
homes to comfort and console him.

JOB 2:11 NIRV

As one whom his mother comforts,
so will I comfort you.

ISAIAH 66:13 AMP

S.O.S.

Doreen hadn't come out of her house for days. When the telephone rang, she ignored it. Friends dropped by, but she just said she was busy and shut the door. They had no clue that her husband had just left her for another woman. This was a private matter, Doreen reasoned. God was there with her. With His help, she felt certain she could handle whatever lay ahead, no matter how painful.

Indeed, God was there for Doreen; but in her attempt to "handle" life on her own, she missed the comfort He longed to extend to her. She missed words of encouragement and support. She could only receive those blessings by opening herself up to the love of her friends.

Asking for prayer and the support of others isn't a sign of weakness. It's the way God intended it to be—growing strong by leaning on each other. Where do you turn when you need help?

You don't have to be alone in your hurt. Comfort is yours. Joy is an option.

The Lord waits for you to come to him,
so he can show you his love.

ISAIAH 30:18 TLB

They cried to the Lord in their trouble,
and he delivered them from their distress;
he made the storm be still, and
the waves of the sea were hushed.

PSALM 107:28-29 RSV

But without faith it is impossible to
please him: for he that cometh to God
must believe that he is, and that he is a
rewarder of them that diligently seek him.

HEBREWS 11:6 KJV

Prayer is totally fat-free.

Innocent Obsession

Dark, light, truffle, solid, or filled . . . Alicia wasn't particularly choosy about her obsession, just as long as it was chocolate. She kept a box hidden in her desk at work, one in the pantry at home, and one in the freezer for emergencies.

It was only 8:30 A.M., but Alicia's in-box already contained enough new work to keep her busy through the end of the week. She reached for her secret stash, then stopped. She knew she turned to chocolate when she was depressed, tired, frustrated, lonely, or stressed. *Maybe I should reach for something that could actually change the way I'm feeling,* she speculated. Then she bowed her head and took a few moments to ask God for His help.

What do you turn to when life's a struggle? What do you reach for to fill the emptiness inside? Remember, a moment with God is better than the finest chocolate.

Watch out that no bitterness takes root
among you, for as it springs up it causes deep
trouble, hurting many in their spiritual lives.

HEBREWS 12:15 TLB

Whatever is noble . . . right . . .
pure . . . lovely . . . admirable—
if anything is excellent or praiseworthy—
think about such things.

PHILIPPIANS 4:8 NIV

(God) forgive us our sins, just as we have
forgiven those who have sinned against us.

MATTHEW 6:12 NIRV

Weed Eater

"It's too bad you can't afford a maid," Lena said, with a bittersweet smile. "It must be hard keeping up the house with two kids underfoot." The gray-haired woman took a sip of tea and added, "Of course, I had four children and my house was always 'spic and span'. We had a different work ethic back then."

Carmen found her mother-in-law's caustic words echoing through her head, like so many similar conversations they'd had in the past. But this time, Carmen decided to do something about it. She reached into the deepest part of her heart, and with God's help, pulled up her resentment firmly by the roots.

Rehearsing hurt in your mind plants the seeds of bitterness. When this persistent weed takes root, it chokes the love out of relationships. The first step to uprooting bitterness is refusing to hold a grudge. Are there any roots you need to pull today?

If you hug to yourself any resentment against anybody else, you destroy the bridge by which God would come to you.

Commit your way to the Lord.

PSALM 37:5 NIV

This is the day the Lord has made.
We will rejoice and be glad in it.

PSALM 118:24 NIRV

Teach us to number our days,
that we may gain a heart of wisdom.

PSALM 90:12 NKJV

Life in the Fast Lane

Today Barbara's calendar looked more like a battle plan than a planner. Appointments spilled out of the box marked "Tuesday." Personal notes with red arrows filled every available margin. Barbara sighed and transferred her schedule onto a larger sheet of paper. Ordinarily, she left breathing room in her day, but sometimes things snowballed. And today, if one appointment ran long, or if Barbara was caught in traffic, that snowball would cause an avalanche.

So, Barbara took one of her very valuable minutes to bow her head and commit her day to God. She realized that His plans for her might look a lot different than the list on this piece of paper, and she didn't want to miss His still, small voice amidst the hustle and bustle.

Simply wait upon Him. So doing, we shall be directed, supplied, protected, corrected, and rewarded.

Each day, from the most extraordinary to the most ordinary, isn't really in your hands, but God's. This is true whether you commit it to Him or not.

The Lord detests the sacrifice of the wicked,
but the prayer of the upright pleases him.

PROVERBS 15:8 NIV

Prayer offered in faith will heal the sick.

JAMES 5:15 NIRV

For we are glad, when we are weak,
and ye are strong: and this also
we wish, even your perfection.

2 CORINTHIANS 13:9 KJV

*A mother's prayers are the wings
that help her children fly.*

Letting Go

Stuffed animals, CDs, photo albums, and what seemed like a mall's worth of clothing—it looked as though her daughter was finally ready to go. "Bye, Mom! See you at Thanksgiving!" With that, Connie's daughter drove off into the sunset.

Connie wasn't sure how Erin could possibly be leaving for college. In her mind, her daughter was still four, playing with mud pies. Or, perhaps she'd made it to thirteen, donning her first pair of nylons for a school dance. But nineteen? Connie shuddered to think what that meant about her own age.

As she watched Erin drive around the corner, she whispered, "Please go with her, Lord." But she already knew He was there; that's why Connie could turn around and walk back inside with a peaceful heart.

God is with those we love, even when we can't be. Whom do you need to pray for across the miles right now?

There is a time for everything, a season
for every activity under heaven.

ECCLESIASTES 3:1 NLT

He has made everything beautiful in its time.

ECCLESIASTES 3:11 NIV

A wise man's heart discerns
both time and judgement.

ECCLESIASTES 8:5 NKJV

Living the Good Life

Cleaning house was Ellen's least favorite task each week. Laundry she could handle. Cooking involved a bit of creativity. But, cleaning? It was drudgery, plain and simple. Still, it had to be done, week after monotonous week. As Ellen began to dust the family photos, just as she did every Friday about this time, something about her son's smile prompted her to pray for him, for the problems he was facing at school.

As she finished with the photo, she picked up the ashtray. She thanked God that now only dust, instead of ashes, covered it. She asked God to give her husband the strength he needed to quit for good this time. As she dusted the clock, she thanked God for the time He'd given her, forty-four years and counting.

God can be found in even the most mundane moments of life. Better yet, He can turn them into time well spent.

When it comes to life, the critical thing is whether you take things for granted, or take them with gratitude.

The Lord your God is with you,
he is mighty to save.

ZEPHANIAH 3:17 NIV

For in the day of trouble He will hide me
in His shelter; in the secret place
of His tent will He hide me;
He will set me high upon a rock.

PSALM 27:5 AMP

To trust in the Lord means safety.

PROVERBS 29:25 NIRV

Close Call

Out of the corner of her eye, Gail saw the blur of a red truck. In a split second, she realized it would run the light. As the words, "God, no!" escaped from her lips, everything seemed to move in slow motion—Gail hit the brakes; her car strained to stop; and the truck swerved, missed her by inches, then sped down the road as if nothing had happened. Her heart raced as she pulled over to the curb to catch her breath.

While her adrenaline seemed to continue to brace for the worst, Gail found herself rejoicing in the best—the fact that she was alive and unhurt. It was a blessing she'd taken for granted just moments before, and now she was filled with a renewed appreciation for how precious life was—and how fragile. As she resumed her commute, her heart couldn't stop giving thanks.

How has God's protection touched your life today?

Being prayerful is as important as being careful.

Say to those with fearful hearts, "Be strong,
do not fear; your God will come."

ISAIAH 35:4 NIV

My eyes are ever looking to the Lord for help,
for he alone can rescue me.

PSALM 25:15 TLB

I will say of the Lord,
"He is my refuge and my fortress;
My God, in Him I will trust.

PSALM 91:2 NKJV

*Only he who can say, "The Lord
is my strength," can say,
"Of whom shall I be afraid?"*

Test of Courage

When the nurse mentioned an MRI, Gloria began to panic. It wasn't the results of the test she feared but the thought of being shoved into that little tube. Small spaces had always terrified her. As a kid, she couldn't even play hide-and-seek without being concerned that her wildly beating heart would give her away. She knew it was irrational, but that didn't make her fear any less real.

As the test began, Gloria closed her eyes and pictured God at her side, holding her hand and making sure there was enough air for her to breathe. Then she began to pray for all of the friends she knew were praying for her. She began to sing praise songs in her mind, and she repeated the Twenty-third Psalm. In those moments, her anxiety was replaced with peace.

If you're facing a frightening situation in your life, keep your mind on God. He'll see you through.

Let us not become weary in doing good,
for at the proper time we will
reap a harvest if we do not give up.

GALATIANS 6:9 NIV

Give your burdens to the Lord.
He will carry them. He will not permit
the godly to slip or fall.

PSALM 55:22 TLB

Don't be afraid, for I am with you.
Do not be dismayed for I am your God.
I will strengthen you.

ISAIAH 41:10 NIRV

Persevering in Prayer

By noon, Janet could tell the day was going to be a "doozy." Most people didn't understand what it was like to have a son with bipolar disorder. They just assumed Janet couldn't keep Jason under control. But she was learning to find encouragement in her son's little victories—a homework assignment turned in, a morning without an argument, the rare invitation to a birthday party.

Janet sighed. She'd lost count of how many times she'd prayed for God's help this morning. She constantly looked to God for guidance and support, and He assured her with small triumphs along the way. God had entrusted Jason to her care, and His faith in her was enough to keep her going. She knew that she would spend the rest of her life in gaining strength from God for her son.

Do you have a challenging circumstance in your life? Give it to God—one moment at a time.

You haven't failed until you've quit.

We know that suffering produces
perseverance; perseverance,
character; and character, hope.

ROMANS 5:3-4 NIV

You have turned for me
my mourning into dancing;
You have put off my sackcloth
and clothed me with gladness.

PSALM 30:11 NKJV

O Lord, thou art our father;
we are the clay, and thou our potter;
and we all are the work of thy hand.

ISAIAH 64:8 KJV

Unlikely Treasure

"**Y**our grandmother wore this on her wedding day, just as I did on mine," Anne's mother said wistfully, placing the strand of pearls around her daughter's neck. "Today, they're yours."

Anne looked at the milky white strand and smiled. "It's hard to believe these were once just grains of sand," she said, stifling an unexpected giggle during this solemn moment. "Think how many oysters had to get irritated so I could feel beautiful!"

Her mother laughed with her, but thought about the pain she had suffered bringing Anne into the world. God had transformed that terrible pain by covering it with layers of love until its form had totally changed, and the pain forgotten. Now she was about to give away her pearl of great price to another. Time seemed to stand still as she looked into her daughter's eyes.

Both darkness and light give sunrise its beauty.

Sometimes God's best gifts are wrapped in pain. If you're in pain today, ask God to unwrap yours.

We all stumble in many ways.

JAMES 3:2 NIV

Why do you pass judgment on your
brother? Or you, why do you despise
your brother? For we shall all stand
before the judgment seat of God.

ROMANS 14:10 RSV

Do not make any hasty or
premature judgements.

1 CORINTHIANS 4:5 AMP

*Relationship is a dance
where it's easy to step on
one another's toes.*

Blowing It

Paula ducked back out the restaurant door, her face flushed with anger. Before she had left the office, she had asked her friend Jean to join her for lunch, but Jean had said she was too busy. Now Jean sat enjoying lunch with a woman Paula had never met. Jean had lied to her!

In a split second, Paula reclassified Jean from friend to traitor. How could she ever trust her again? Since she had lost her appetite, she returned to the office without eating. When Jean walked by her desk later and said hi, she just nodded without smiling, pretending she had too much work to do.

Paula was still fuming inside when she overheard two co-workers talking about how nice it was of Jean's sister to drop in from out of town to surprise her. Paula's anger quickly turned to shame. "Lord, forgive me," she prayed.

Are you too quick to draw conclusions?

Defend your people, Lord; defend and bless
your chosen ones. Lead them like a shepherd
and carry them forever in your arms.

PSALM 28:9 TLB

I can do everything through him
who gives me strength.

PHILIPPIANS 4:13 NIV

Be of good courage, and He shall strengthen
your heart, all you who hope in the Lord.

PSALM 31:24 NKJV

Facing the Impossible

The drone of the waves lapped the shore like a lullaby. Monica rocked peacefully in her hammock, a tall glass of iced tea in her hand. But a pesky parrot continued to cry out from a nearby palm tree. Monica covered her ears, but it wouldn't go away. It wasn't until her husband shook her awake that she realized her baby's cry had worked its way into her dreams. Feeding time, again.

Monica knew mothers had done this for centuries, but as she stumbled sleepily into the nursery, she found herself feeling resentful toward the little child she loved so much. As she fed the baby, she began to cry. The tears were born of love and frustration, as well as a desperate need for a moment alone. "Lord, please give me strength tonight," she prayed, and she immediately sensed His presence.

Whom do you turn to for strength when you feel overwhelmed by the responsibilities of life?

Seven days without prayer makes one weak.

Husbands, in the same way be considerate
as you live with your wives, and treat them
with respect as the weaker partner and as heirs
with you of the gracious gift of life, so that
nothing will hinder your prayers.

1 PETER 3:7 NIV

Timely advice is as lovely as
golden apples in a silver basket.

PROVERBS 25:11 NLT

Let no one seek his own,
but each one the other's well-being.

1 CORINTHIANS 10:24 NKJV

Intimate Encounter

Jeffrey put on Connie's favorite tie, adjusted his jacket, and then headed for the car. Picking up Connie at work was one of his favorite things to do. Catching sight of her waiting for him always made him feel very special. He carefully placed the bouquet of yellow roses and a funny card, picturing cows on the front, on the passenger seat.

Connie reapplied her lipstick and gave her hair a quick comb. Jeffrey would be here any moment, and she wanted to look her best. She'd made reservations at their favorite restaurant. The manager knew to put them in the back because they'd be sitting there for hours, just talking. They'd been married twenty-nine years, yet they still had many things to learn about each other.

Chains do not hold a marriage together. It is threads, hundreds of tiny threads that sew people together through the years.

The way to keep love fresh is to always keep asking questions, giving compliments, and discovering each other's faith in God.

For it is God who works in you both
to will and to do for His good pleasure.

PHILIPPIANS 2:13 NKJV

We do not lose heart. Though outwardly
we are wasting away, yet inwardly
we are being renewed day by day.

2 CORINTHIANS 4:16 NIV

God began doing a good work in you.
And he will continue it until it is finished
when Jesus Christ comes again.

PHILIPPIANS 1:6 NCV

*Who we are becoming is
as important as who we are.*

Common Threads

Scraps piled up all over Shawna's workroom. From a distance, it looked like chaos. But Shawna knew the story behind every piece of fabric: the satin binding from a baby blanket . . . the square of velvet from a prom dress . . . the calico swatch from a favorite doll's dress. With her daughter's impending graduation from college, it was time to join the pieces into a quilt.

Although Shawna had quilted for years, she was always amazed at how patterns and colors that seemingly clashed could end up looking as though they belonged together. *Just like our lives,* she thought. *I can't wait to see the quilt God's making from my scraps.*

Are there times when your life looks like a handful of scraps, faded and fraying? God wants to take those scraps and stitch them into a beautiful quilt just for you. Will you let Him?

The Lord is compassionate and gracious,
slow to anger, abounding in love.

PSALM 103:8 NIV

"Now I will relieve your shoulder
of its burden. I will free your hands
from their heavy tasks." He said,
"You cried to me . . . and I saved you."

PSALM 81:6 TLB

God is our refuge and strength,
always ready to help in times of trouble.

PSALM 46:1 NIRV

Under Control

Mona looked around her house with satisfaction. The CDs were alphabetized. The sheets were washed and pillowcases pressed. Even the wicks on her candles were trimmed. After all, she knew that too long a wick could make a candle burn too hot, causing the wax to melt quickly and unevenly.

Just like my temper. The thought entered Mona's mind unexpectedly, leaving her flushed with shame. Her home may have been under control, but she knew her emotions were far from it. She tried to hide her anger and appear loving, but in her heart, she knew she was a fraud. None of her other strategies worked, either. She hadn't changed at all. Prayer was her only hope. "Lord," she asked, "show me how to surrender and what it means to 'let go and let God.'"

How are you handling your emotions? Is your temper acting up? God can help, if you let Him.

The heart is God's workshop, but only you can let Him in.

I run in the path of your commands,
for you have set my heart free.

PSALM 119:32 NIV

Be diligent to present yourself
approved to God.

2 TIMOTHY 2:15 NKJV

Search me, O God, and know my heart;
test my thoughts. Point out anything
you find in me that makes you sad.

PSALM 139:23-24 TLB

The Road to Freedom

The flashing lights in Talia's rear-view mirror sent her heart into panic. She glanced at her speedometer. Reassured she was going the speed limit, she pulled over. The police car quickly darted past her in pursuit of some unknown emergency. Talia pulled back into traffic, breathing more easily.

She wondered how anyone could habitually break the speed limit. She knew she'd be a nervous wreck. She preferred following the rules and relaxing, instead of driving everywhere with one eye on the rear-view mirror, hoping she wouldn't be caught.

What about your relationship with Paul? The thought seemed to come from nowhere and pierced her heart. Her face flushed. Paul had asked her to spend the weekend with him, and she was on her way to his apartment. In that moment, she vowed not to compromise her values again. Looking in her rear-view mirror, Talia turned the car around.

A guilty conscience can be a ticket to change.

Have you been compromising?

Do your best, prepare for the worst—
then trust God to bring victory.

PROVERBS 21:31 THE MESSAGE

Do not be afraid or terrified . . .
for the Lord your God goes with you.

DEUTERONOMY 31:6 NIV

Be strong and of good courage; be not
frightened, neither be dismayed; for the
Lord your God is with you wherever you go.

JOSHUA 1:9 RSV

*The best way to stand up for
what's right is on your knees.*

The Right Stuff

When it came to confrontation, Joanne's approach wasn't exactly that of an iron fist. A wet noodle was more like it. Some people she confronted never even realized what she was doing. Quiet by nature, she was more comfortable not making waves. But she was trying to change and speak up when she needed to.

So when Joanne felt God prompt her to speak to her boss about some major discrepancies in his expense report, she prepared for the meeting on her knees. She wanted to get the facts straight and recognize her expectations. She wasn't there to fix anything; that was God's department. Outside of her boss's door, she took a deep breath, willed her shaking knees to stop knocking, and rapped on the door. When he indicated she should enter, she whispered a last, quick prayer before opening the door.

Where do you find the courage you need to do the right thing?

Each of you must take responsibility
for doing the creative best
you can with your own life.

GALATIANS 6:4-5 THE MESSAGE

Forgetting what is behind and straining
toward what is ahead, I press on toward
the goal to win the prize for which
God has called me heavenward.

PHILIPPIANS 3:13-14 NIV

Show me the path where I should go, O Lord;
point out the right road for me to walk.

PSALM 25:4 TLB

Moving On

The whistle of the teakettle continued for several minutes. Rebecca hardly noticed, reflecting on the familiar images in her hands. The focus of her attention wasn't anything new. Almost every morning since she had moved across country from her family, one of her numerous photo albums sat in her lap. Some days, she could hardly gather the strength to put it away.

But this morning was different. Rebecca asked God to join her for a going-away party. She took one last look at her albums before storing them in the attic. It was time to make this new city her home—to make new friends and new memories. She'd lived in the old ones for too long. She said good-bye to each of the faces in the album and prayed God would help her take the first step toward whatever lay ahead.

God is good at drying our tears and putting a new song in our hearts.

You don't have to forget something to leave it behind.

I will not forget you! See, I have engraved
you on the palms of my hands.

ISAIAH 49:15-16 NIV

Revive my heart towards you.
Reassure me that your promises are for me.

PSALM 119:37 TLB

The Lord will command His
loving-kindness in the daytime, and in
the night His song shall be with me.

PSALM 42:8 AMP

Unforgettable

Robin searched the lost-and-found box with a sense of futility. Although it was overflowing with hats, gloves, a couple of tattered jackets, and even a dirty sock, she was fairly sure her scarf was history. Purple chenille with sage-green fringe—it was exactly what she had asked her sister Carla to knit for her. Carla had a talent for those artsy kinds of things. But just a week later, Robin lost it.

"I wonder if there's a greeting card that says 'thank you' and 'I'm sorry' at the same time?" Robin lamented. "It's a good thing God isn't as absent-minded as I am. Lord, please help me find it."

"Is this what you're looking for?" the attendant asked, holding up her scarf.

"Yes!" she exclaimed. As she wrapped the scarf around her, she thanked God that He even cared about the little things in her life.

God could never lose those He holds in His hand.

God cares about the little things, and the big things in your life, as well.

Keep steady my steps
according to thy promise.

PSALM 119:133 RSV

My God turns my darkness into light.

PSALM 18:28 NIV

Blessed is the people that know the
joyful sound: they walk, O Lord,
in the light of thy countenance.

PSALM 89:15 KJV

*God is the Lighthouse that
will always beckon you home.*

Wandering in the Wilderness

Brenda and camping went together like chiffon and burlap—not an attractive ensemble. Her kids loved the idea of sleeping outside, and her husband seemed as at home in a tent as he did in his favorite easy chair. So Brenda tried to be a good sport. Unfortunately, her idea of "roughing it" was a hotel without a built-in blow dryer.

At least the campsite had a bathroom just down the trail. But Brenda's flashlight batteries were fading fast. Everything looked unfamiliar in the darkness, and she couldn't tell which direction she was headed. "Mitch!" she called out with an edge of desperation. "Where are you guys?" A flashlight beam and her husband's voice broke through the darkness. All it took was a little light, and Brenda easily found her bearings again.

Living without God is like finding your way in the darkness without a flashlight. Call out to God, and ask Him to shine the light of His love on your path.

If the Lord delights in a man's way,
he makes his steps firm.

PSALM 37:23 NIV

His lord said to him, 'Well done, good and
faithful servant; you have been faithful over a
few things, I will make you ruler over many
things. Enter into the joy of your lord.'

MATTHEW 25:23 NKJV

Give your bodies to God.
Let them be a living sacrifice.

ROMANS 12:1 TLB

The Perfect Part

As the curtain went down, the parents' applause filled the auditorium. Emily was good-naturedly pushed out onto the stage to receive a bouquet of flowers and words of thanks for her work in putting together the production. Although she was much more comfortable behind the curtain than in front of it, she also had a few words of thanks to give. She thanked God for the courage to take on something bigger than she could pull off on her own.

Emily always pictured a leader as someone filled with confidence and authority—someone gruff and tough. Her personality was just the opposite. But when she was asked to head up the student presentation, she had felt God's peace in saying yes. From there on out, she watched God take her common talents and use them in remarkable ways.

Are you allowing God to use your talents for His glory?

With God, human efforts can have divine results.

I cry out to God Most High, to God,
who fulfills his purpose for me.

PSALM 57:2 NIV

Look at the birds, free and unfettered,
not tied down to a job description,
careless in the care of God. And you
count far more to him than the birds.

MATTHEW 6:26 THE MESSAGE

And the very hairs on your head are
all numbered. So don't be afraid.

MATTHEW 10:30-31 NIRV

Death of a Dream

"You tricked me!" Joan cried. She had never spoken to God like she was doing right now, but she was angry. After all, she'd quit a great job and moved across country to work at a church, of all places. It had only been four months, and now her position had been cut. All Joan wanted was to serve God. Now what?

The only thing she could think to do was pray, even in her anger. But first, she had to tell God how she really felt.

Following God had not been a carefree journey for her. There had been plenty of stops and starts and seemingly meaningless detours. As she prayed, she realized that it all came down to trust. Either she trusted God to fulfill His plan for her life, or she didn't. Even though life didn't make sense right now, she decided to trust Him.

Sometimes, God's way from point A to point B ends up going through X, Y, and Z.

Are you committed to trusting God, even when the circumstances don't make sense?

Come to me, all you who are weary and
burdened, and I will give you rest.

MATTHEW 11:28 NIV

As for me, my contentment is not
in wealth but in seeing you and
knowing all is well between us.

PSALM 17:15 TLB

As a deer pants for streams of water,
so my soul pants for you, O God.

PSALM 42:1 NIV

*If you're too busy to spend time
with God, you're too busy.*

Overwhelmed and Under-prayed

Carol searched for a clear surface where she could set the bags of groceries. Finding nothing, she finally dropped them on the floor. Sighing, she surveyed the chaos that surrounded her. Yesterday's dishes filled the sink because the dishwasher hadn't been emptied from two nights before. A basket of clean laundry sat on the couch, waiting to be folded, and dirty laundry crept out of the laundry room door. Carol didn't know where to begin.

When life became busy, the first thing she neglected was her time with God. He knew what she was facing, she reasoned. He'd understand. But that morning, Carol realized that time with God was what she needed most. She sat down on the bottom stair and began to pray. "Forgive me, Lord, for treating my relationship with You as if it's just another chore to be crossed off my list. Give me strength to tackle whatever the day holds." She felt better immediately.

Walk before me in integrity of heart.

1 KINGS 9:4 NIV

People with integrity have firm
footing, but those who follow
crooked paths will slip and fall.

PROVERBS 10:9 NLT

May integrity and honesty protect me,
for I put my hope in you.

PSALM 25:21 NIRV

Missteps

Erin rolled over and stared at the clock for one last time before finally climbing out of bed. Another sleepless night. *"When am I going to stop this?"* she wondered. Then groggily, she showered, dressed, and headed out the door to work.

"You look terrible," said Barb, who was never much for subtlety. "What's wrong?"

"I'm just not sleeping much, that's all." Erin knew that wasn't all, but she was embarrassed for her best friend to know the truth.

"Erin, can we talk?" Barb responded with a look of concern Erin hadn't seen on her face before. "What's really going on? Is something wrong?"

Erin swallowed hard. She was tired of living two lives. Maybe it was time to come clean. *Dear God,* she prayed silently, *I don't know if You're still listening, but if You are, please give me the strength to be truthful.* "Barb, I have a problem," she began.

Being honest is always the first step to receiving the help you need.

The steps on the stairway to integrity are too far apart for you to reach without God's assistance.

And he said to him, "Rise and go your way;
your faith has made you well."

LUKE 17:19 RSV

Therefore Eli said to Samuel, "Go, lie down;
and it shall be, if He calls you, that you must
say, 'Speak, Lord, for Your servant hears.'"
So Samuel went and lay down in his place.

1 SAMUEL 3:9 NKJV

Then Peter said, "Silver and gold I do not
have, but what I have I give you. In the
name of Jesus Christ of Nazareth, walk."

ACTS 3:6 NIV

Skywriting

Kate stared into the cloud-filled sky, wishing God would give her a clear answer. "I think you should take it, Kate. Kate?"

"Sorry," Kate said, "Do you ever wonder, Stace, why God doesn't do miracles anymore? How hard would it be to make those clouds spell out 'Take the job' or 'Don't take the job'?"

"God still does miracles," her friend replied. "We just don't always recognize them. Besides, I already told you what to do!"

"Yeah," Kate groaned, "but I don't want to move away from my friends."

"It's a great opportunity," Stacey said, "and you'd only be a couple of hours away. Have you heard of this new thing called the telephone? It works wonders for long-distance friendships."

God often uses the people around you to deliver an answer to your prayer.

Kate laughed. Stacey was so wise. Suddenly, she understood. "I get it! You're my skywriting. God sent you to help me with this decision."

"I guess that makes me a little miracle?"

Kate smiled and said, "No, Stace, you're a big miracle."

We all have happy memories of good men
gone to their reward, but the names
of wicked men stink after them.

PROVERBS 10:7 TLB

The Lord preserves the faithful.

PSALM 31:23 NKJV

He will not be moved forever; the
[uncompromisingly] righteous (the
upright, in right standing with God)
shall be in everlasting remembrance.

PSALM 112:6 AMP

*When you look back at the life of a
faithful person, take some of what
you see and look forward with it.*

You've Done Well

"You've done well, Lily." Those words, sent from the bottom of Pastor Jeff's heart to the depths of Lily's soul, captured second place on her list of favorite things. First on that list would be when Jesus says to her in Heaven, "Well done, good and faithful servant." And, at eighty-seven, Lily knew that time was coming soon.

Pastor Jeff had made certain she'd leave behind a legacy. "You have so much to offer," he said to her more than fifteen years ago. That's when she had started teaching the Bible. Then five years ago, he offered to help her write a devotion book. "I know many people will be blessed by it," he'd said.

Lily almost forgot Pastor Jeff was still in the hospital room with her. "I'm tired now, Pastor," she said.

"As you rest, Lily, countless women are being inspired by the devotions you wrote," he replied. But Lily was already asleep.

You're never too old to use your talents for God.

This promise is for you. It is also for your children, and for all who are far away. It is for everyone the Lord our God calls to himself.

ACTS 2:39 NCV

He who fears the Lord has a secure fortress, and for his children it will be a refuge.

PROVERBS 14:26 NIV

I will pour out my Spirit and my blessings on your children. They shall thrive like watered grass, like willows on a river bank.

ISAIAH 44:3-4 TLB

God Bless the Child

The setting sun filled the sky with glorious hues of pink, red, and coral. But Stan and Betty missed it all. They spent the evening just as they had spent many evenings before, kneeling beside the olive green ottoman in the family room, beseeching God to deliver their daughter Angie from drug addiction.

They never expected to find themselves in this situation. They raised their children in a home filled with God's love. But Angie went looking for trouble, and found it. Stan and Betty were confused and hurt, but they never gave up on their prayer vigil.

Months went by, and then one night, Angie called from a treatment center in a nearby city. Her treatment had been involuntary and her recovery slow, but God had used her circumstances to force her to make critical decisions about her life.

Do you have a wayward child? Ask for God's help, and keep asking.

Prayer is invading the impossible.

He heals the heartbroken and
bandages their wounds.

PSALM 147:3 THE MESSAGE

My flesh and my heart may fail, but
God is the strength of my heart
and my portion for ever.

PSALM 73:26 RSV

The Lord is close to the brokenhearted
and saves those who are crushed in spirit.

PSALM 34:18 NIV

The Gift of Love

Gordon and Lucy met late in life. Both had lost their mates—Lucy's husband to a heart attack, and Gordon's wife to cancer. For the first few months, they basked in the excitement of a growing friendship and the sweetness of falling in love. But when it came time to make a commitment, Gordon suddenly backed away. "I'm sorry," he told Lucy. "I just can't take the risk. The possibility of losing another person I love is just too scary for me."

"I'm afraid too," Lucy confessed. "But it seems to me that God has given us a great gift. He's given us someone to share the rest of our lives with." Gordon didn't overcome his fear right away, but with time, he gave his fears to God and took Lucy's hand.

Has the fear of pain and loss kept you from receiving the love and comfort of those God has placed in your life? Give Him your fears and walk into the light of a new day.

He who fears to suffer, suffers from fear.

We plan the way we want to live,
but only God makes us able to live it.

PROVERBS 16:9 THE MESSAGE

Unless the Lord builds the house, they labor
in vain who build it; Unless the Lord guards
the city, the watchman stays awake in vain.

PSALM 127:1 NKJV

Many are the plans in a man's heart,
but it is the Lord's purpose that prevails.

PROVERBS 19:21 NIV

*The only good plans are those that
rely upon the Master Planner.*

Subject to Verification

If the world had a "best planner" competition, Fran would certainly draw a high seed. No one planned like Fran. A quick glance at her wall-sized calendar in the kitchen, and you'd be ready to give her the gold medal without seeing her competitors.

Three years of vacation days were planned out in red. Two months' worth of meals were described in green. Shopping days were described in orange. Television shows (blue), movies (pink), and bowling nights (yellow) were all listed with detailed information. But there was a note at the top of Fran's calendar that put a unique spin on her world. It read: "All dates and details subject to verification by God."

God wants you to make plans—perhaps not as detailed as Fran's. But He wants you to look ahead—to think about tomorrow. It is only by God's goodness that we get to live out those plans. Make sure God is a part of them.

Whatever I have, wherever I am,
I can make it through anything in
the One who makes me who I am.

PHILIPPIANS 4:13 THE MESSAGE

Godliness with contentment is great gain.

1 TIMOTHY 6:6 NIV

I have learned how to get along happily
whether I have much or little.

PHILIPPIANS 4:11 TLB

Modest Circumstance

The tiny stove only had two working burners— enough for spaghetti and sauce, or hot dogs and beans. Melody wasn't sure which meal Carmen would serve tonight, but it didn't matter. She made each one with equal enthusiasm. As Melody knocked on the apartment door, she wondered how she would survive in a two-room, rundown apartment.

"Come on in, hon. I've made you a special dinner tonight." That meant spaghetti. Though she often felt guilty for having so much when Carmen had nearly nothing, Melody still loved visiting her because she was always so thankful. "Thank you, God, for blessing my life so richly," Carmen prayed, as always. Today, they talked about gardens, even though Carmen's apartment was on the seventh floor.

Melody had a lot to learn. Her friend knew everything there was to know about gardens. But more than that, she knew about content-ment. Perhaps that's why Melody contin-ued to visit.

How contented are you?

Contentment makes poor men rich; discontent makes rich men poor.

God doesn't want us to be shy with his gifts,
but bold and loving and sensible.

2 TIMOTHY 1:7 THE MESSAGE

Give, and it will be given to you.
A good measure, pressed down,
shaken together and running over.

LUKE 6:38 NIV

Give as freely as you have received.

MATTHEW 10:8 TLB

Wake Up to Singing

Jerry awakened to singing just about every Saturday morning. His wife, Helen, enjoyed her weekday work—though teaching's rewards were often not realized until years after the children graduated. But Saturday was a day for her family, instead of her students, to feel the warmth and encouragement that flowed like a fountain from her.

Helen sang everything from hymns to rock and roll. It didn't matter, really. She was an encouraging person, and the sound of her joy-filled voice was enough to start the day off right. During the weekdays, her uplifting words fed the starving hearts and minds of teenagers. "Middle school students are the toughest to teach," she once said to a friend. "That's because they need more encouragement."

God's gifts may look like fine china, but they're meant to be used like everyday dishes.

But it was Saturday, and Helen was singing again. Jerry thanked God for giving his wife the gift of encouragement. It was just what those students—and he—needed.

Has God given you a gift that you could share with others?

Live carefree before God;
he is most careful with you.

1 PETER 5:6-7 THE MESSAGE

❧

I will walk in freedom, for I have devoted
myself to your commandments

PSALM 119:45 NLT

❧

Where the Spirit of the Lord is, there is liberty
(emancipation from bondage, freedom).

2 CORINTHIANS 3:17 AMP

*God gives us freedom, not so
we'll run from harm, but so
we'll run to Him with open arms.*

Dancing

Daniel watched, mesmerized, as the woman moved across the stage. Usually, dancing wasn't his thing, but this performer was special. She seemed to dance so freely, with little or no inhibition. "She's good—real good," he heard several audience members whisper.

That's when it hit him—why he'd been so taken by her dancing. Everyone else had seen it too. They all longed to live freely—to dance like children in a field of flowers before God. And so they danced along with her, straining for a taste of that freedom.

You may not express your deepest feelings through dance. Perhaps you sing, play an instrument, paint, write poetry, or do something even more unique. As you perform, think of God as the only Person in the audience, and simply express yourself to Him through your gift. You will be surprised how the freedom you experience will enhance the quality of your performance.

He wraps you in goodness—beauty eternal.
He renews your youth—
you're always young in his presence.

PSALM 103:5 THE MESSAGE

The silver-haired head is a crown of glory,
If it is found in the way of righteousness.

PROVERBS 16:31 NKJV

I will pour out my Spirit on all people . . .
old men will dream dreams.

JOEL 2:28 NIV

Park Bench Memories

Iris visited the park dozens of times while her grand-children were young. But this was the first time she'd returned since moving to the retirement home in Arizona, seventeen years ago. The same park bench she used to sit on while watching Maxie and Tyler still occupied a prime spot under the giant maple tree. She thought about Maxie, who was now living in New York, fighting her way into the fashion industry. And she smiled as she watched Tyler riding the teeter-totter with his young son.

Tyler walked over and sat down next to his grand-mother. "I think Ben likes this place," he said, as Ben rolled down the hill.

"You used to do that, too," Iris said.

"I loved coming here with you, Grandma. Don't ever grow old, okay?"

"Not a chance, Ty," she answered.

If you love God, you're always on the edge of eternity. Eighty-seven is just a pup compared to forever.

Youth is the gift of nature, but age is a work of art.

Put your mind on your life with God.
The way to life—to God!—is vigorous and
requires your total attention.

LUKE 13:24 THE MESSAGE

In the same way, you should be a light
for other people. Live so that they will
see the good things you do [and] will
praise your Father in heaven.

MATTHEW 5:16 NCV

Set an example for the believers in speech,
in life, in love, in faith and in purity.

1 TIMOTHY 4:12 NIV

Role Reversal

Stephanie idolized her big sister, Sherrie, a straight-A student, scholarship magnet, and beauty queen. She was good at everything. Sherrie was Stephanie's inspiration.

But when Sherrie went away to college, she pretty much gave up on God. "Don't have much time for that anymore, Steph," she said, during a rare Internet chat. Stephanie loved her big sister, but putting a relationship with God in the "if I have time" box didn't sit well with her.

Many years later, while visiting her younger sibling, Sherrie said, "I've messed up a ton in my life, but I want you to know I'm changing all that. In fact, I want to thank you."

"Thank me?" Stephanie said. "For what?"

Good example has twice the value of good advice.

"While you were in high school, I looked up to you, Sis. You took your relationship with God seriously. I didn't and paid the price. But you never gave up on me, and now I'm back."

The earth is filled with his tender love.

PSALM 33:5 TLB

I can always count on you—
God, my dependable love.

PSALM 59:17 THE MESSAGE

Your love, O Lord, reaches to the heavens,
your faithfulness to the skies.

PSALM 36:5 NIV

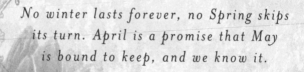

*No winter lasts forever, no Spring skips
its turn. April is a promise that May
is bound to keep, and we know it.*

Change of Heart

The lawn crunched beneath Maggie's feet. Winter had taken its toll. Everything was brown and dry from months of snow and frost. She reached down to pick up a nearby leaf, a lone reminder of fall. It crumbled in her fingers. The tree branches were skeletons of their springtime selves. Maggie's heart felt right at home with the season—dormant, searching for signs of new growth.

"God, if I could just see a sign of spring, it would mean so much," she whispered under her breath. But everything seemed gray and lifeless—not a bud, not a bird, not a hint of green anywhere. It wasn't time, and Maggie knew it.

Though it is often bleak, winter isn't a sign that God no longer cares about the earth. The same is true when we experience times of winter in our hearts. Often, it's just a season when growth goes underground—and a glorious spring will follow.

For You have been a strength to the poor,
A strength to the needy in his distress,
A refuge from the storm, A shade from
the heat; For the blast of the terrible
ones is as a storm against the wall.

ISAIAH 25:4 NKJV

He who has pity on the poor lends
to the Lord, and that which
he has given He will repay to him.

PROVERBS 19:17 AMP

Generous people will be blessed, because
they share their food with the poor.

PROVERBS 22:9 NCV

Long Distance Love

Trash heaps are no place for children to play, let alone live. Jenna put the brochure from the relief organization down on the table and picked up her checkbook. As she slipped her donation into the envelope, she couldn't stop the flow of words headed toward Heaven: "God, how can You let this kind of stuff go on in the world? Where are You? Please help these children. Your blessings to me have been too generous, and theirs, too few."

As Jenna prayed, God brought to mind not only the check she'd just written, but also how her heart had been moved to pray. Indeed, God provided for these children, and He used Jenna in the process.

God didn't create us to be self-sufficient. People were designed to be dependent on God and each other. That interdependence is where we learn what love really is.

It is ours to offer what we can, God's to supply what we cannot.

Let your gentleness be evident to all.

PHILIPPIANS 4:5 NIV

But when the Holy Spirit controls our lives,
he will produce this kind of fruit in us:
love, joy, peace, patience, kindness, goodness,
faithfulness, gentleness, and self-control.
Here there is no conflict with the law.

GALATIANS 5:22-23 NLT

Let not yours be the outward adorning
with braiding of hair, decoration of gold,
and wearing of fine clothing, but let it
be the hidden person of the heart with the
imperishable jewel of a gentle and quiet spirit,
which in God's sight is very precious.

1 PETER 3:3-4 RSV

Quiet Strength

Bonnie watched with curiosity as the kindergartners flocked around Debra the moment she arrived. During story time, whoever had the privilege of sitting in Deb's lap was the envy of the class. Bonnie's lap, on the other hand, was always second choice. Bonnie tried to be loving. She tried playing games, giving piggyback rides, and to make the kids laugh. It wasn't that the kids didn't like her; but she was just another teacher's aide. Debra was a kid magnet.

Bonnie continually asked God to help her accept the inability to be best at everything. Over time, she came to recognize there was something special about Debra's tenderness. It made her lap, and just her presence, feel like a quiet brook, welcoming others to lie beside it and rest.

There is nothing stronger than gentleness.

Gentleness can be just as evident in strength as it is in a word of blessing or a gesture. It isn't docile or complacent. It's power tempered by love.

I have learned to be content whatever the circumstances.

PHILIPPIANS 4:11 NIV

Remember what Christ taught and let his words enrich your lives and make you wise; teach them to each other and sing them out in psalms and hymns and spiritual songs, singing to the Lord with thankful hearts.

COLOSSIANS 3:16 TLB

Let your conduct be without covetousness; be content with such things as you have. For He Himself has said, "I will never leave you nor forsake you."

HEBREWS 13:5 NKJV

Counting someone else's blessings, instead of your own, divides gratitude and multiplies discontent.

Satisfaction Guaranteed

Bologna on white bread with two cookies—Johnny's lunch looked pretty good. Or, it had just a moment ago. Now, it was as appealing as a bowl of "kibble." That's because right across the lunch table, Casey Cartwright's mom had just brought pizza to school for him—hot pepperoni pizza with extra cheese. It wasn't Casey's birthday or anything. She brought it just because.

Soon, not only was Johnny's lunch looking bad, so was his mom. She never brought him pizza. Why, some days she even asked him to pack his own lunch. *And those cookies? Not even homemade.* What kind of life was he living? He wished he were Casey Cartwright. Then he could really be happy.

Whether we're children at school or adults at our jobs, comparison and discontent go hand-in-hand. God's plan for your life will look different than His plan for anyone else's. And you can rest assured that God's plan is exactly right for you.

You will call, and the Lord will answer;
you will cry for help, and he will say,
"Here am I."

ISAIAH 58:9 NIV

God's there, listening for all who pray,
for all who pray and mean it.

PSALM 145:18 THE MESSAGE

Keep company with God, get in on the best.

PSALM 37:4 THE MESSAGE

Unlikely Sanctuary

It wasn't an easy chair by the fireplace. But on those crazy days when the kids seemed to attach themselves like lichens onto the pant legs of her jeans, Chris headed for the bathroom and locked the door. It was only for a few minutes, but that was enough to help her get through the morning with her emotions and sanity in check.

"Dear, Lord," she began. "Here I am again with just the usual stuff. Please help me know what to do and what to leave undone. And help me share Your love with my kids, even when I don't feel very loving. Thanks. Amen."

God's ready to meet you anytime, anyplace. You don't have to book an appointment or set aside an entire afternoon. He longs to hear what's going on in your heart. A moment with God can help readjust your priorities and remind you that you're not alone.

Little do men perceive what solitude is, and how far it extendeth.

God promises to love me all day, sing songs
all through the night! My life is God's prayer.

PSALM 42:8 THE MESSAGE

The LORD is my strength and
my song; he has become my victory.
He is my God, and I will praise him;
he is my father's God, and I will exalt him!

EXODUS 15:2 NLT

I will sing to the Lord,
for he has been good to me.

PSALM 13:6 NIV

In the Child's Song

"Jesus loves me, this I know, for the Bible tells me so. . . ." Sally's sweet voice wafted into the kitchen through the open window. Bonnie looked out at her five-year-old. After singing six more songs, Sally suddenly grew quiet. Seconds later, she ran, breathless, into the kitchen and said, "Mom! Guess what?"

"What, Honey?"

"I was just singing to God, and all of a sudden, I heard God singing too!"

Bonnie smiled at her young daughter and said, "Maybe you heard me through the window—I was humming along with you."

Sally scrunched up her face. "No, Mommy. It wasn't you. I heard God singing."

Rather than argue, Bonnie decided to play along. "I enjoyed your singing. Maybe God was enjoying it, too, and wanted to sing along. What did He sound like?"

God is knowable, touchable, hearable, seeable, with the mind, the hands, the ears, and eyes of the inner man.

"Well, at first He sounded like the wind—but then like a bird. He has a real pretty voice."

God's love . . . you can feel it in the wind, smell it in a flower, hear it in a bird's song.

Open up before God, keep nothing back;
he'll do whatever needs to be done.

PSALM 37:5 THE MESSAGE

The Lord is close to the brokenhearted.

PSALM 34:18 NIV

Life rooted in God stands firm.

PROVERBS 12:3 THE MESSAGE

*God doesn't make broken
hearts as good as new—
He makes them NEW.*

Shattered

The plate slipped from Sandra's hands and shattered on the tile floor. She stood there for a moment, stunned. Then the tears began to flow. The plate had been her mother's, one of the only reminders Sandra had of her. Now it was gone, broken beyond repair. The fine china looked like colorful flowered shards scattered beneath her feet.

And nothing can put Humpty-Dumpty together again, she thought. As the nursery rhyme ran through her head, her heart wrote an alternate ending—*except God.* Looking at that plate reminded her of how she'd felt when her mother died—broken, useless. But God had put her back together. Even though the plate was gone, Sandra's memories were intact. Better yet, so was her heart.

Brokenness is a consequence of life, but that doesn't mean you should become accustomed to the pain. God is not only close to the brokenhearted, He also heals them.

Sow for yourselves according to righteousness
(uprightness and right standing with God);
reap according to mercy and loving-kindness.
Break up your uncultivated ground, for it
is time to seek the Lord, to inquire for
and of Him and to require His favor.

HOSEA 10:12 AMP

The point is this: he who sows sparingly
will also reap sparingly, and he who sows
bountifully will also reap bountifully.

2 CORINTHIANS 9:6 RSV

Be not deceived; God is not mocked:
for whatsoever a man soweth,
that shall he also reap.

GALATIANS 6:7 KJV

Spreading Seeds

The smell of damp, freshly tilled soil was perfume to Vivian. It beckoned her into the garden with the promise of a quiet morning spent encouraging things to take root and grow. Her friends were convinced plants loved to grow for her because, over time, her tiny plot of ground would turn into a piece of paradise.

Vivian knew a beautiful garden was more than a matter of luck. She couldn't plant weeds and expect rose bushes. It took careful planning, hard work, and time. "What you plant is what you get," she always told her friends. And since she tended her friendships as well as her garden, she reaped much love as well as beautiful blooms.

"Bloom where you're planted" is good advice. But wherever God plants you, you'll be doing more than blooming. You'll be planting seeds. What grows in your life, and in the lives of those you touch, will reflect the type of seeds you plant.

To own a bit of ground, to scratch it with a hoe, to plant seeds, and watch their renewal of life—this is . . . the most satisfactory thing a man can do.

Those who trust in riches will be ruined. But a
good person will be healthy like a green leaf.

PROVERBS 11:28 NCV

Though your riches increase,
do not set your heart on them.

PSALM 62:10 NIV

Because you have trusted in your wealth
and skill, you will be taken captive.

JEREMIAH 48:7 NLT

Dollars and Sense

As Gina sat down to pray, her sister was the first person she thought of. No matter what she tried, Colleen proved successful. She'd even joked the word "failure" was not a part of her vocabulary: until now. The Internet company she started so successfully last year was seriously floundering. That morning, Colleen was moving out of the new house she'd recently bought.

Gina knew her sister's situation wasn't life or death. But she also knew, from Colleen's point of view, the loss of her house could feel like the lost of a spouse. Maybe this is exactly where God wants her, Gina thought. Instead of praying for financial recovery, she found herself praying that God would do whatever it took to reach Colleen's heart.

You don't have to be rich to trust in your riches. Money can buy a lot, but a life that's rich with God's blessing isn't for sale.

What you have never determines your true worth.

But they that wait upon the Lord shall renew
their strength. They shall mount up with wings
like eagles; they shall run and not be weary;
they shall walk and not faint.

ISAIAH 40:31 TLB

Though he (God) slay me, yet will I hope in him.

JOB 13:15 NIV

Yea, let none that wait for thee be
put to shame; let them be ashamed
who are wantonly treacherous.

PSALM 25:3 RSV

*They travel lightly whom
God's grace carries.*

Tired of Trying

The pounding of the bass reverberated through the house, drowning out the sound of the oven timer. It had been buzzing for over an hour, but Paula was frantically cleaning house. That meant the stereo was cranked full blast. When she finally remembered the brownies, she knew it was too late. At this point, they'd make a more appropriate doorstop than a dessert.

When she opened the oven door, she burst into tears. She had been trying so hard to do everything right. The stupid brownies reminded her of her heart—fried. "God, I can't do it anymore," she prayed. "Everything feels so out of control."

Right then, she decided to rearrange her day. She gave up on the homemade dinner and ordered pizza for her company, instead. With the time she had left, she went for a walk to chat with God about the priorities in her life.

Whom do you turn to when your day seems out of control?

Who of you by worrying and being anxious
can add one unit of measure (cubit) to
his stature or to the span of his life?

MATTHEW 6:27 AMP

Do not worry . . . Look at the birds of the air;
they do not sow or reap or store away in barns,
and yet your heavenly Father feeds them.
Are you not much more valuable than they?

MATTHEW 6:25-26 NIV

So don't worry about tomorrow.
Each day has enough trouble of its own.
Tomorrow will have its own worries.

MATTHEW 6:34 NCV

Hurried Worries

Joyce was a champion worrier. She worried about her children so emphatically during their elementary school years that she would show up twice a week at school just to make sure they were okay. That was in addition to the three days she already volunteered in the classroom.

When her children went on to junior high and high school, she continued to keep close tabs on everything they did and everywhere they went. It was only a minor surprise when she had a heart attack at forty-four years of age. When the news reached her now college-age children, they raced back to the hospital to visit.

They barely entered the room when Mom spoke up through the oxygen mask, "You don't need to worry—I'm going to be fine."

In unison, they responded, "Look who's talking!" Strong-worded threats from doctors to take it easy, and her children's wise advice, reduced Joyce's worrying substantially.

Worry never robs tomorrow of its sorrow, it only saps today of its strength.

But sanctify the Lord God in your hearts,
and always be ready to give a defense to
everyone who asks you a reason for the hope
that is in you, with meekness and fear.

1 PETER 3:15 NKJV

Do not let any unwholesome talk come of
your mouths, but only what is helpful for
building others up according to their needs.

EPHESIANS 4:29 NIV

Let your conversation be gracious as well
as sensible, for then you will have
the right answer for everyone.

COLOSSIANS 4:6 TLB

Shared Hope

Chatting with Monica always felt like a breath of fresh air to Janice. On the outside, their lives looked identical: married, two small kids, husbands with good jobs—the American Dream. But on the inside, Janice cried out for more. She wasn't sure if she needed to have a part-time job, go to counseling, or win the lottery.

Maybe she needed God. She knew that's what Monica would say. Monica talked about God like He was right there in the room with them. Janice often wondered if He really was. Something about Monica's life was different from her own, despite all the similarities. Monica seemed to find genuine joy in little things, contentment even when life was downright ordinary. And when her husband lost his job last year, she didn't panic; she prayed. When she talked with her, Janice always knew something was missing in her own life. She decided to talk to Monica about God again.

One of the greatest evidences of God's love to those who love Him is that He sends them grace to bear afflictions.

The greatest thing you could ever do is to show and tell your friends about the love and grace of God.

Before they call I will answer;
while they are still speaking I will hear.

ISAIAH 65:24 NIV

The Lord's promise is sure. He speaks no
careless word; all he says is purest truth,
like silver seven times refined.

PSALM 12:6 TLB

I love the Lord because he hears my prayers
and answers them. Because he bends down and
listens, I will pray as long as I breathe.

PSALM 116:1-2 TLB

*To believe in God is to know that
all the rules will be fair—and that
there will be wonderful surprises!*

A Treasure Beyond Shoes

Ceil was on her way home, feeling blue. After intensive testing, she and her husband received the news that their chances to conceive children were slim. They considered adoption. But this was all new thinking, and it seemed overwhelming. She had cried out to God for direction, but nothing seemed clear.

Then she saw it: Shoe SALE—50% to 80% off! Ceil loved shoes. And there was nothing she liked better than a shoe sale. She made her way down the racks.

"I can't believe it," she said out loud. "My favorite brand, 75% off."

A woman turned to her, saying, "I know, they're the best!" Ceil then noticed, as she always did, a little one in the carriage. The woman lifted the awning to reveal a beautiful baby boy.

"This is Nicholas. My husband and I just adopted him from Russia—" And there, right in that shoe department, Ceil found God's answer and began the incredible journey into parenthood.

It is more blessed to give than to receive.

ACTS 20:35 NLT

Good people give without holding back.

PROVERBS 21:26 NCV

Freely you have received, freely give.

MATTHEW 10:8 NIV

Boomerang Blessing

To Jessica, turning sixteen was something worth celebrating. From getting her driver's license in the morning, until her first boy-girl party that evening, she was the center of attention. And that felt good.

But turning forty was something different altogether. Jessica no longer had to be the center of attention to feel good. That's why she planned her own backward birthday celebration. She invited friends and family to join her, specifying on the invitation, "No gifts, please." Then she wrote thank-you notes to give to each of her guests, expressing how their lives had made her own so much richer. Attached was a small "birthday" gift—a reminder of some memory they'd shared together.

Though her intention was to bless others, the party itself reminded her of the incredible blessings she received from others throughout the years. She'd never received a more perfect gift (not even at her sixteenth birthday party).

When was the last time you thanked those who have made your life richer?

The only gift is a portion of thyself.

In the multitude of my [anxious]
thoughts within me, Your comforts
cheer and delight my soul!

PSALM 94:19 AMP

Trust in him at all times, O people; pour out
your hearts to him, for God is our refuge.

PSALM 62:8 NIV

As one whom his mother comforteth,
so will I comfort you.

ISAIAH 66:13 KJV

Across the Chasm

The cliff's edge seemed the perfect place to sit and contemplate the news. "I feel as far from you right now, God, as this edge of the cliff is from the other side," Rachel said, as she stared across the chasm.

Any other day, she'd have been overwhelmed by the beauty of the sunset and the meandering river far below. But not today. Rachel, instead, was overwhelmed by this world: injustice in Africa, a killer earthquake in India, and—betrayal by her best friend. "Where are you, God?" she called out across the canyon. Her voice echoed a few seconds, then died away. She began to cry.

Then, she sensed a faint sound returning to her, and she knew that she was not alone; God was in those echoes.

People often fail us, but God never will. That doesn't make the betrayal of a friend less painful, but it does give us Someone dependable to go to for comfort.

Providence has at all times been my only dependence, for all other resources seem to have failed us.

Do not be far from me, for trouble
is near and there is no one to help.

PSALM 22:11 NIV

I want you to trust me in your times of trouble,
so I can rescue you, and you can give me glory.

PSALM 50:15 TLB

Even when walking through the dark valley of
death I will not be afraid, for you are close
beside me, guarding, guiding all the way.

PSALM 23:4 TLB

*We need never shout across the spaces
to an absent God. He is nearer
than our own soul, closer than
our most secret thoughts.*

Temperamental Truth

Yolanda felt she'd been on an emotional roller coaster for the last week. That was to be expected with everything she was going through. But what she didn't expect was to feel so far from God. Especially, because she'd felt so close to Him only yesterday. Where had He gone? She got on her knees for the third time that day. Even if she couldn't feel God, she knew He was the only One she could turn to right now, so she continued to reach out, even when she felt there was no One reaching back.

The intimacy of God's presence is a wonderful thing. But on this earth, it's most likely a fleeting experience, not a perpetual state. How you feel about something isn't an accurate gauge of the truth. When your emotions say that God is far away, remind yourself of what is true—that God is always with you, and that nothing can separate us from His love.

Don't be afraid. I am with you.
Don't tremble with fear. I am your God.

ISAIAH 41:10 CEV

The Lord is my light and my salvation—
whom shall I fear?

PSALM 27:1 NIV

What time I am afraid, I will trust
in thee. In God I will praise his word,
in God I have put my trust; I will not
fear what flesh can do unto me.

PSALM 56:3-4 KJV

Vanquishing Fear

Karen finished her grocery list, placed her checkbook and coupon holder in her pocketbook, and slipped to her knees next to the sofa. "Lord," she prayed, "please give me the courage I need to leave the house today." She waited there quietly until she felt God's strength uplift her and His peace calm her fears.

Karen's request helped her deal with a disorder known as agoraphobia, the gripping fear of public places. In the year since her husband's death, the condition kept her housebound, isolated in sorrow and grief. Finally, help came in the form of a wonderful counselor who introduced her to God and suggested that prayer could provide the courage she needed to keep her fear and panic at bay.

You may not suffer from the terror of agoraphobia, but the remedy Karen chose can help you conquer other anxieties that plague your life. Offer your fears to God, and wait quietly for His enabling power.

Courage is resistance to fear, mastery of fear— not absence of fear.

Count it all joy, my brethren, when you meet
various trials, for you know that the testing
of your faith produces steadfastness.

JAMES 1:2-3 RSV

If you do not stand firm in your faith,
you will not stand at all.

ISAIAH 7:9 NIV

You shall weep no more, for he will surely
be gracious to you at the sound of your cry.
He will answer you.

ISAIAH 30:19 TLB

Trial Number Twenty-four

"Trial seventeen: Dishwasher is spewing soapy suds on the kitchen floor. Eighteen: Must be at work two hours early tomorrow. Nineteen: Husband working late again. Twenty: Toilet overflowing. Twenty-one: Water from toilet dripped into the basement. Twenty-two: Slipped on kitchen floor. Twenty-three: Sister complained I missed her birthday. Twenty-four: To Be Decided . . ."

Jane's journal entry for this Tuesday rivaled all others for the number of challenges faced in one twenty-four-hour period. On days like this, she usually held so tightly to the prospect of some spiritual benefit from the trials that she practically served up a challenge to face more. "C'mon, I can take it," she would boast.

But this Tuesday, she felt defeated. "Please, God, no more trials," she prayed. Thankfully, no trials worth noting followed her plea. As the day finally winded down, she went to her journal one more time. "Trial number twenty-four: Ran out of energy to see trials as a good thing. God took over from there."

Adversity can either destroy or build up, depending on our chosen response.

They cried out to God during the battle,
and he answered their prayer
because they trusted in him.

1 CHRONICLES 5:20 NLT

The Lord has heard my cry for help.
The Lord will answer my prayer.

PSALM 6:9 NCV

The prayer of the upright is His delight!

PROVERBS 15:8 AMP

*Prayer requires more of the
heart than of the tongue.*

Prayer Protocol

Ordering pizza by phone prompted Jackie to pray. She found it difficult to communicate, especially with strangers. Most of them tried to be polite, but her stuttering made the most casual conversation waver between uncomfortable and impossible.

But when Jackie prayed, she knew God wasn't in a hurry for her to finish a sentence. He had all the time in the world. That's one reason she often prayed aloud, to remind herself that even when the words she was trying to say refused to come across perfectly, God understood. He loved her just the same.

How you sound when you pray doesn't matter to God. You may have the vocabulary of an evangelist, or a child. You may pray confidently in front of a group, or never have spoken a prayer aloud in your life. It's all the same to His ears, for He hears your heart.

For God wanted them to wait and share the even better rewards that were prepared for us.

HEBREWS 11:40 TLB

Your beginning will seem humble, so prosperous will your future be. Though your beginning was small, Yet your latter end would increase abundantly.

JOB 8:7 NIV

Many, O Lord my God, are the wonders you have done. The things you planned for us no one can recount to you.

PSALM 40:5 NIV

The Waiting Dress

Jane was furious. "You're calling off the wedding, just like that!" she yelled through the phone to her fiancé. "You don't think we're right for each other—oh, I see. You might have mentioned that before we bought and sent the invitations and before my parents spent a fortune on my wedding dress!" In her anger and frustration, she kept asking, "Why?"

She believed she was hurt beyond repair. *How could he do this with no warning?* she thought. She cried on her mom's shoulder, looking at the perfect wedding dress hanging high in the corner of her room. God, how could You have let this happen? she questioned. Months passed, and the daintily pearled dress hung in the basement, a reminder of the perfect plan that had come apart at the seams.

Then she met Rick. This was something she'd never experienced. She returned home from their second date, somehow knowing that her dress would be worn. Now, God, I see.

God has a perfect plan for every life.

God's gifts put man's best dreams to shame.

Not by might, nor by power, but by
my Spirit, says the LORD of hosts.

ZECHARIAH 4:6 RSV

In returning and rest shall ye
be saved; in quietness and in
confidence shall be your strength.

ISAIAH 30:15 KJV

Is not by sword or spear that the Lord saves;
for the battles is the Lord's.

1 SAMUEL 17:47 NIV

Growing Strong

The fall day had a slight nip in the air, but the warmth of the sun overpowered it. It was the perfect day for a hike through the canyon. After an hour or so, Rebecca told her friends she'd catch up with them. She wanted to spend a few moments alone with God to enjoy the beauty that surrounded her. As she took a drink out of her canteen, her eyes caught sight of an evergreen tree growing out of the side of the sheer cliff wall.

I can't even get herbs to grow in pots on my protected windowsill, she thought in amazement. Somehow that seed fell into enough soil to thrive. *I guess God just wanted it there.* Rebecca reflected on how God had the same plan for her life. Unwanted as a child, she was adopted into a great family. Now, she couldn't imagine growing up anywhere else. Indeed, God grows great lives under less-than-ideal circumstances.

Before God created the universe, He already had you in mind.

Humble yourselves therefore under
the mighty hand of God, that
in due time he may exalt you.

1 PETER 5:6 RSV

❧

I desire to do your will, O my God;
yes, your law is within my heart.

PSALM 40:8 NIV

❧

Your will be done on earth
as it is in heaven.

MATTHEW 6:10 NIV

*To will the will of God in himself and
for himself and concerning himself is
the highest possible condition of a man.*

No Front Page Story

The alarm went off like a banshee and screamed until Cindy crawled out of bed and turned it off. The shower's cold spray attacked her like a thousand icy bullets before the hot water kicked in.

She wrestled the door from the howling wintry wind, and stepped into the still-dark morning to begin her mile-long trek to the nursing home. With that, Cindy began her day—a day that would feature dirty bedpans, messy sponge baths, and grumpy patients. Still, it was a job, and she did it adeptly and patiently.

Sometimes her patients would smile or say thanks. And in those moments, she knew she made a difference. In the moments she wasn't so sure, she continued to keep a cheerful attitude. Either way, she knew she was doing the work, for a time, that God had given her to do—and that was all that mattered.

Are you living and working in the center of God's will?

When the Lord saw her, He had compassion
on her and said to her, "Do not weep."

LUKE 7:13 NKJV

You will grieve, but your grief will turn to joy.

JOHN 16:20 NIV

Your sun shall no more go down, nor your
moon withdraw itself; for the LORD will
be your everlasting light, and your
days of mourning shall be ended.

ISAIAH 60:20 RSV

The Thing About Grief...

She should get on with her life by now, Sarah thought about her co-worker Jean. It had been six months since Jean lost her husband. At first, she had seemed to be fine. She came back to work two weeks after the funeral. But now, she seemed to regress—falling apart and crying in meetings. She was apologetic, and others seemed to understand. But secretly, Sarah thought she was wallowing.

Then Sarah's grandmother passed away. It was a pain she had never felt before—a physical knot in her stomach that wouldn't subside. And Sarah, usually not prone to tears, would cry at the oddest times. One of those times, she was talking to Jean. "I never imagined . . ." she sobbed.

Jean put an arm around her and said, "Honey, you go ahead and cry. I understand. And God does too."

Don't judge those who are grieving. Offer them, instead, your love and kindness, as well as God's.

Grief can be your servant, helping you to feel more compassion for others who hurt.

He defends the cause of the fatherless.

DEUTERONOMY 10:18 NIV

Sing to God, sing praises His name,
cast up a highway for Him Who rides
through the deserts—His name is the Lord—
be in high spirits and glory before Him!
A father of the fatherless and a . . . protector
of the widows is God in His holy habitation.

PSALM 68:4-5 AMP

The Lord your God, who is going before you,
will fight for you, as he did for you in Egypt
. . . There you saw how the Lord your God
carried you, as a father carries his son.

DEUTERONOMY 1:30-31 NIV

Metamorphosis

Watching Lori walk down the aisle in her wedding gown brought Trisha to tears. It wasn't because she looked so beautiful and had fallen in love with such a wonderful guy. Rather, it was because Lori walked down the aisle with her father on her arm— something Trisha would never be able to do.

Growing up without a father was difficult for Trisha. Her mom was a remarkable woman, but there was always that feeling she missed out on a father's love. This was one of those times. But, as Trisha pictured herself walking down the aisle, there was Someone on her arm. *I'll be walking right beside you. Just as I always have,* she heard God say. And His reassurance made her tears flow even more. Now they were tears of joy.

Do you long for a father's love? Remember that your Heavenly Father loves you more than any earthly father ever could.

In His love he clothes us, enfolds us and embraces us; that tender love completely surrounds us, never to leave us.

The mind controlled by the
Spirit is life and peace.

ROMANS 8:6 NIV

I am leaving you with a gift—peace of
mind and heart! And the peace I give isn't
fragile like the peace the world gives.
So don't be troubled or afraid.

JOHN 14:27 TLB

Do good; seek peace, and pursue it.

PSALM 34:14 KJV

*Peace is not the absence
of conflict from life, but
the ability to cope with it.*

A Moment of Peace

The highway appeared to be a parking lot again—the fifth time in five days. Laura never enjoyed the drive to work. Now it would take an extra hour. A broken air conditioner meant open windows. Open windows meant exhaust fumes.

She would be late to her 9:00 morning meeting—with the company president. If only she had charged her cell phone overnight. Carting the kids all around town had kept her too busy to remember to plug in the phone.

The stress of the moment should have overcome Laura. It would have, a few months earlier. Today, though, she was relaxed. The world wouldn't end because of a highway delay. All would be well. She must have smiled because other motorists stared at her with quizzical looks. She just smiled and thanked God for teaching her to release her stress to Him.

Are you stressed out by the circumstances of your life? Pause for a moment, and release your stress to God.

I have loved you with an everlasting love.

JEREMIAH 31:3 NIV

For your unfailing love is
higher than the heavens.
Your faithfulness reaches to the clouds.

PSALM 108:4 NLT

Because thy steadfast love is better than life,
my lips will praise thee.

PSALM 63:3 RSV

Benediction

"If I should die before I wake, I pray the Lord my soul to take." Hannah finished with a quick "Amen," and then bounced her way under the blankets. "Mommy, why would God take my soul?" Hannah asked with wide-eyed innocence.

Rhonda's eyes welled up with tears. Then she tried to tell her daughter a little about Heaven, downplaying death to avoid nightmares. But as she kissed her goodnight and turned off the light, Rhonda realized she didn't want to talk about death for her own sake, not Hannah's. Since the day Hannah was born, she had been afraid something would happen to her. She felt it was her job to protect her, even from God. Right then, Rhonda stood outside Hannah's door, voicing a prayer of her own—a prayer of love and release.

Place the lives of those you love into the hands of a God. It isn't easy. But the truth is, there is much freedom in entrusting those you love to an all-knowing, all-loving God.

Rest assured, God's love is even greater than your own.

The only accurate way to understand ourselves
is by what God is and by what he does for us,
not by what we are and what we do for him.

ROMANS 12:3 THE MESSAGE

Long before he laid down earth's foundations,
he had us in mind, had settled
on us as the focus of his love.

EPHESIANS 1:5 THE MESSAGE

Save me in your unfailing love.

PSALM 31:16 NIV

The Source of Love

Kara tried to be sensitive. She was always kind and tried not to let anyone down. She figured out what rubbed people the wrong way, and then did the exact opposite. Being likable wasn't a bad thing, she reasoned. After all, she did everything in the name of love.

Until one day, when Kara over-committed herself into a corner because she thought that saying no would have been impolite. As a result, reliable Kara let others down. They forgave her, but forgiving herself was another matter. That day, God showed her that the person she was really trying to love was herself. It was a painful revelation, but it changed the way she related to God, others, and herself. She finally understood what real love was all about.

What makes you "valuable?" Is it what you do? What you have? Who you know? No, you are valuable because God created you, knows you intimately, and loves you completely.

Our acceptance before God is complete and secure even when we are disappointed in ourselves.

May He grant you according to your heart's
desire and fulfill all your plans.

PSALM 20:4 AMP

Many, O LORD my God, are thy wonderful works
which thou hast done, and thy thoughts which are
to us-ward: they cannot be reckoned up in order
unto thee: if I would declare and speak of
them, they are more than can be numbered.

PSALM 40:5 KJV

But the plans of the Lord stand firm forever.

PSALM 33:11 NIV

*What God sends is always better
than what people ask for.*

The Big Plan (vs. the Little Ones)

Things had not gone as Gina planned. She had wanted a quiet spring break, but her roommate, Amy, talked her into a visit to the Big Apple. Amy said she had a cousin they could stay with, so Gina reluctantly agreed. She thought a vacation together might be difficult because she liked to plan her days, and Amy was the "let's see what happens" type.

Unfortunately, she was right, and now they were on the last ferry to Ellis Island. Gina preferred to have gone earlier, so she could find her family's name in the immigration records, but it hadn't worked out. She moved to the upper deck to get some air. Then, she leaned over, looking toward the Statue of Liberty. Suddenly, someone bumped her. "Sorry," he said, and smiled. In front of her was the man whom God wanted her to meet—and spend the rest of her life with. In the first five minutes of their conversation, somehow, she knew it. She thought she was running late, but God's timetable is always perfect.

When our plans are submitted to God's plan, we can always expect the best.

God is my help.

PSALM 54:4 NIV

❧

God is our refuge.

PSALM 62:8 NLT

❧

God is my strength.

PSALM 73:26 NCV

❧

Mistaken Identity

When Bess heard an old friend had moved into town, she couldn't have been happier. She looked forward to a heartfelt reunion with Chris, catching up on old times and planning future adventures together. A mutual friend at work had Chris's address, which she gave to Bess. Wanting to surprise her old friend, Bess decided to knock on Chris's door, unannounced.

After finding no one at home for several days, Bess finally heard footsteps in response to her fervent knock. When the door opened, her excitement turned to confusion. A stranger stood in the doorway. "You must have the wrong address," the woman said.

Are you looking for God but are confused by what you find? You might be knocking at the wrong address. Are you expecting God to be the ultimate Santa Claus? Superhero? Policeman? Spend some time getting to know the God of the Bible. It's hard to build a relationship with Someone you can't recognize.

Sincerity isn't a reliable road to truth.

The Lord has delivered you today.

2 SAMUEL 18:31 NIV

The Lord protects the simple
and the childlike.

PSALM 116:6 TLB

You are a hiding place for me; You, Lord,
preserve me from trouble, You surround me
with songs and shouts of deliverance.

PSALM 32:7 AMP

Timely Exit

It was May's second-to-last day of work. Leaving was bittersweet. She'd miss the job and the people, but she welcomed the fact that she would no longer have to commute fifty miles. In a rare show that seemed out of character, the CEO told her to take her "last day" off, with pay. And May wasn't going to argue with that.

The next day was rainy and foggy—a good time to rest and relax. Later in the day, she sank into the couch to catch the news—*this is just about the time I'd be heading home,* she thought smugly. For a second, she couldn't believe what she heard—a forty-car pile-up, right where she would've been, right at that time. "Thank you, God," she said. On her couch, still in her pajamas, she prayed for the people on the road.

Even when we don't know it, God is watching over us, protecting and keeping us safe.

Faith reposes on the character of God, and if we believe that God is perfect, we must conclude that His ways are perfect also.

My grace (My favor and loving-kindness and mercy) is enough for you [sufficient against any danger and enables you to bear the trouble manfully]; for My strength and power are made perfect (fulfilled and completed) and show themselves most effective in [your] weakness.

2 CORINTHIANS 12:9 AMP

The Lord gives me strength and makes me sing. He has saved me. He is my God, and I will praise him. He is the God of my fathers, and I will honor him.

EXODUS 15:2 NCV

Seek the Lord and His strength; Seek His face evermore!

1 CHRONICLES 16:11 NKJV

God can make you anything you want to be, but you have to put everything in His hands.

Jackpot

"Go fish!" Teresa's six-year-old was delighted to see her mom pick up card after card, until she could barely hold them all. It was just a kid's game, but it felt more like Teresa's life. Growing up without a dad: pick up a card. Her teenage pregnancy: pick up a card. Her husband walking out: pick up a card. Overdue bills: pick up a card. Losing her job: pick up a card. Teresa realized she had made her share of mistakes, but she also felt God had given her more than she could handle.

"I win!" her daughter shouted, merrily gathering the cards to begin another hand. As Teresa threw her cards on the table, she realized that's exactly what God wanted her to do. Instead of grumbling over the hand she'd been dealt, she needed to acknowledge that God was the only One who could hold everything she was trying to hold.

Are your cards in your hands, or in God's capable hands?

The Lord himself is my inheritance, my prize.

PSALM 16:5 TLB

He will always give you all you need from
day to day if you will make the Kingdom
of God your primary concern.

LUKE 12:31 TLB

Where does my help come from?
My help comes from the Lord,
the Maker of heaven and earth.

PSALM 121:1-2 NIV

Heritage of Faith

A garage sale seemed an almost disrespectful way to sell family heirlooms. But Wendy was out of choices—and money. As a polyester-pant-clad woman picked up her grandmother's favorite teapot, Wendy almost grabbed it out of her hands. But, hospital bills needed to be paid.

What would my relatives think? Wendy wondered. As she helped a man put her father's golf clubs into his car, she prayed for strength. God answered with a memory. Her father always compared prayer to the perfect caddy, handing you just the right club to handle whatever lay ahead. He told her, "All you need do is ask." An unexpected smile came across Wendy's face. All of this stuff was just stuff. What was really of value was safe within her heart.

Are your circumstances requiring you to make difficult choices? Look to God. He is always ready to help.

Learn to hold loosely all that is not eternal.

Acknowledgements

Abraham Joshua Heschel (7), Clement of Alexandria (11), W. D. Gough (13), Jewish Proverb (21), Hannah Hurnard (25), Malcolm Muggeridge (29), Saint Augustine of Hippo (33), Charles Dickens (39), Saint John Chrysostom (41), Oswald Chambers (43), Philip James Bailey (45), F. B. Meyer (47), Leigh Nygard (51), Henry David Thoreau (53), The Berdichever Rabbi (57), Billy Zeoli (59), Eugene Gladstone O'Neill (65), Robert Murray McCheyne (73), Joni Eareckson Tada (75), Peter Marshall (79), Vance Havner (81), G. K. Chesterton (85), Alexander MacLaren (89), Simone Signoret (99), Jack Hayford (127), Spanish Proverb (129), Benjamin Franklin (133), Garson Kanin (139), Hal Borland (143), Saint Jerome (145), Francis Bacon (151), A. W. Tozer (153), Charles Dudley Warner (157), Thomas Á. Kempis (161), Archibald Joseph Cronin (163), Sister Corita (167), Ralph Waldo Emerson (169), George Washington (171), A. W. Tozer (173, Tim Hansel (177), Adam Clarke (179), Elizabeth Barrett Browning (181), Edwin W. Lutzer (183), George MacDonald (185), Robert Harold Schuller (187), Julian of Norwich (189), Edwin W. Lutzer (195), A. W. Tozer (201), Mahalia Jackson (203), Agnes Maude Royden (205).

Additional copies of this book and other titles
from this series are available
from your local bookstore.

Glimpses of an Invisible God
Glimpses of an Invisible God for Teens

If you have enjoyed this book,
or if it has impacted your life,
we would like to hear from you.

Please contact us at:

Honor Books
Department E
P.O. Box 55388
Tulsa, Oklahoma 74155
Or by e-mail at info@honorbooks.com